CHRONOL
THE HOLY FACE DEVOTION
History, People, Places, & Prayers

*A historical timeline of the
people & events which took place to fulfill
Our Lord's desire to make
the Holy Face Devotion a reality.*

Compiled and written by Vicki Schreiner
Edited by John J. Schreiner

© 2022 Vicki Schreiner
Simply Faith Publishing
Oklahoma City, OK

Holy Face Adoration & Devotion
www.HolyFaceAdoration.com

*"Rejoice, My daughter, because
the hour approaches when the most
beautiful work under the sun will be born."*
-- Our Lord
To Sister Mary of St. Peter

DECLARATION

We hereby declare that we absolutely and entirely conform to the decree of Urban VIII with respect to the terms of eulogy or veneration applied to the servants of God, Sister Marie Pierre, and Leo Dupont, and other pious persons, as well as to the Divine revelations mentioned in the present book; and, moreover, that we by no means anticipate the decisions of the Holy See.

IMPRIMATURS and ECCLESIASTICAL APPROBATIONS
are listed with each applicable source on pages 144-146

"By My Holy Face You Will Work Wonders..."
-- Our Lord
To Sister Mary of St. Peter

Acknowledgement

To all who practice the Holy Face devotion
for the Reparation of sin
as Our Lord revealed to Sister Mary of St. Peter

Dedication

For my dear family who fill my life with love and joy.
And to the friends I have met through the Holy Face devotion,
who continue to pray for me and this ministry.
I pray with all my heart that Our Lord bless each of you
with His divine mercy and radiant love.

VERA EFFIGIES SACRI VULTUS DOMINI NOSTRI JESU CHRISTI
QUAE ROMA IN SACROSANCTA BASILICA S. PETRI IN VATICANO RELIGIOSISSIME ASSERVATUR ET COLITUR

THE HOLY FACE OF JESUS

True image of the Face of Our Lord Jesus Christ
Venerated in Rome in the Most Holy Basilica of St. Peter

Vicki's family's Holy Face of Jesus holy relic
commissioned by Pope St. Pius X, 1905

Register with the Archconfraternity of the Holy Face in Tours, France:

To this day, you may become a member of the Archconfraternity of the Holy Face by sending a written request to the Oratory:

Centre Spirituel de la Sainte Face
8, rue Bernard Palissy,
37000 Tours, France
Email:
Recteur.oratoiresainteface@gmail.com

The Golden Arrow Prayer
Dictated by Our Lord to Sister Mary of St. Peter

*May the most holy, most sacred, most adorable,
most incomprehensible, and unutterable Name of God,
be always praised, blessed, loved, adored, and glorified,
in heaven, on earth, and in the hells,
by all the creatures of God,
and by the Sacred Heart of our Lord Jesus Christ
in the most Holy Sacrament of the Altar. Amen.*

CONTENTS

PREFACE

My amazing journey for the beautiful Holy Face devotion began early in 2016. My Aunt Catherine, then at the age of 92, had to be placed in a nursing-home due to the onset of severe dementia. As our family emptied the contents from her duplex, we came across the old box containing an image which Aunt Catherine always referred to as "that Jesus picture". Through the years, we never knew what this image was. Our grandmother never spoke of it, and it always remained tucked away in an old box, never to see the light of day. As far as we have been able to ascertain, our family's Holy Face of Jesus engraving came from my great-grandparents who immigrated to Chicago from Trier, Germany (on the border of France and Germany) in the year 1908.

As I began doing extensive research to find information about this image, I discovered that it was an authentic Holy Face of Jesus engraving from the Vatican. At that moment, I was so overwhelmed that I dropped to my knees and cried! Our family had been truly blessed with this holy image that had been commissioned by His Holiness Pope St. Pius X in 1905. The Certificate of Authenticity on the back, written in Latin, verifies that it has been touched to the three instruments of our Lord's Passion; the Veil of Veronica, the True Wood of the Cross, and the Lance that pierced Christ's side.

After over one hundred years of getting knocked around in that old box, the frame had taken a beating. The back was broken and in pieces and the image itself which

9

is printed on holy linen was no longer in the frame. When I took it to a framer to be repaired, he found it extraordinary that the linen image hadn't disintegrated after all the years of exposure it had sustained. I told him that I was certain it had survived due to the fact that it had been touched to the instruments of our Lord's Passion which had been touched to the Blood of Christ.

As I delved deeper into researching this amazing devotion, I felt it was my responsibility to share this holy relic and teach the Holy Face devotion to others. I therefore obtained permission from my family to become guardian of the relic which had remained hidden for so many years. It has been my honor and privilege to travel to churches throughout the US to share this devotion for the past six years.

Due to the onslaught of questions that I receive about the Holy Face devotion, I decided to write this book. In order to make it an easy-to-use learning guide, I've placed in chronological order all of the people, places and events that took place throughout history which finally made this devotion a reality as our Lord desired.

Sadly, it all but disappeared shortly before World War I. Now, in our troubled times, we desperately need this devotion to return and flourish for the reparation of sin. It is my hope and prayer that the Holy Face devotion will wrap around your heart the way it has done mine, and that you will in turn share it with family and friends.

Blessings to you and those you hold dear,

Vicki

It begins...

Our Savior was on the painful journey to Calvary, loaded with the heavy wood of the cross, the altar on which He was to sacrifice His life for the redemption of mankind.[1] He was covered with blood from the scourges which He had received, and the wounds of His blessed temples, which were caused by the crown of sharp thorns.[2] A woman named Berenicia, moved with

---

[1] Veronica; or, The Holy Face of Our Lord Jesus Christ, An Historical Notice of this Most Holy Relic of the Vatican Basilica of St. Peter, London: Thomas Richardson and Son (1870), p.6

[2] Veronica; or, The Holy Face of Our Lord Jesus Christ, p. 7

compassion, braved the fury of the cruel soldiers and also the violent and bloodthirsty populace,[3] removed her veil to help our Lord wipe His face covered with sweat, spittle, dust, and blood. Jesus, after having used it, gave it back to her, having impressed on it His majestic and venerable image, so full of deep sorrow into which He was then plunged by the weight of the sins of the world.[4]

It was only afterwards that Berenicia was known by the name of Veronica, which name is given from the words VERA ICON, meaning "true portrait", to commemorate her brave conduct. The woman named Veronica is no other than the one of whom St. Luke speaks. He represents her to us as afflicted, during twelve years, with an issue of blood which no physician had been able to heal. But she came behind Jesus and touched the hem of His garment and felt immediately that she was cured.[5]

One of our old ascetic authors, full of admiration for this sublime act of Veronica, does not hesitate to place it above even the most sublime examples of virtue which the world has ever witnessed.[6] "The Savior made thee the most precious gift which He has ever bestowed on any earthly creature, for He gave thee His portrait impressed

---

[3] Veronica; or, The Holy Face of Our Lord Jesus Christ, p. 11

[4] Veronica; or, The Holy Face of Our Lord Jesus Christ, p. 6

[5] The Devotion to The Holy Face at St. Peter's of the Vatican and in Other Celebrated Places, by the REV. ABBE JANVIER (1888), p. 12

[6] The Devotion to The Holy Face, JANVIER, p. 16

on thy veil. Spread it then in sight of the four portions of the globe; make all men behold the piteous and disfigured Face of a suffering God. Preach by means of the holy Effigy the Passion of Jesus Christ and make it to reach far beyond the place to which the apostles extended the knowledge of it."[7]

The miraculous veil, impressed with the features of Jesus, could not be allowed to remain as private property. It was a gift of Jesus Christ to His church, a relic destined for the center of Catholicity. Therefore, Veronica took it to Rome.[8]

"Veronica was summoned to depart from Jerusalem and to go to Rome with the Holy Veil by the order of Emperor Tiberius Ceasar...the Emperor was confined to his bed with serious illness… Having placed the precious veil in a reliquary, Veronica arrived at Rome where she was presented to the Emperor. As soon as he had received the holy woman, and had touched the Effigy of the Christ, he was completely cured. In consequence of this miracle, Veronica was held in great esteem by the Emperor."[9]

It is said that Tiberius Ceaser, after his cure, wished to heap favors and riches on his benefactress. But she refused all the offers of the Emperor, knowing well that she possessed a treasure compared with which everything besides was as nothing. She kept it with the

---

[7] The Devotion to The Holy Face, JANVIER, p. 17

[8] The Devotion to The Holy Face, JANVIER, p. 20

[9] The Devotion to The Holy Face, JANVIER, p. 21

utmost care and, afterwards, it became the inheritance and the treasure of the Church. All who testify to it are agreed in saying that she gave the veil to St. Clement.[10]

Pope St. Clement, the third successor of St. Peter, ruled over the church from the year 93 to 102 A.D. During the Persecutions of the first three centuries which beat so terribly against the vessel of the infant Church, Clement and his successors secretly preserved the holy relic in the depths of the catacombs.[11]

In the year 707, Pope John VII, having built an oratory in the Vatican Basilica, which he dedicated to the Blessed Virgin, raised an altar in it in honor of the Holy Face, and placed it there in a beautiful large and ornamental tabernacle with marble pillars.[12]

In the time of Innocent III (1198 - 1216 A.D.), medals were cast with the image of the Holy Face on them, which were called Veronicas.[13]

In the year 1492, Pope Innocent VIII received as a gift from the Emperor of the Turks, the Holy Lance which pierced the side of the Redeemer.[14]

---

[10] The Devotion to The Holy Face, JANVIER, p. 26-27

[11] Veronica; or, The Holy Face of Our Lord Jesus Christ, p. 18

[12] Veronica; or, The Holy Face of Our Lord Jesus Christ, p. 21

[13] Veronica; or, The Holy Face of Our Lord Jesus Christ, p. 15

[14] The Devotion to The Holy Face, JANVIER, p. 41

It was Pope Urbain VIII who had Veronica's Veil deposited in the place which he had destined for it, under the great dome, the masterpiece of Michael Angelo, in the recently constructed basilica of St. Peter. The ceremony took place on the 23rd of December of the holy year 1625. The Holy Face and the Holy Lance, which had been temporarily deposited in the archives of the Basilica and enclosed in an iron coffer covered with a piece of rich damask, were carried in procession and under a canopy to the great niche known as that of "St. Veronica." In order further to increase the veneration of the faithful towards the holy Effigy, Urban VIII decreed that on the

8th of April 1629, there should be added to the Holy Face and Holy Lance, a piece of the Wood of the True Cross. [15]

The three precious Relics are kept at the present day in an oratory situated in the interior of one of the four pentagonal pillars which support the great dome of St. Peter's on the epistle side of the papal altar.

Veronica's Veil in
St. Peter's Basilica

---

[15] The Devotion to The Holy Face, JANVIER, p. 42

The shrine which contains them is ornamented exteriorly with a bas-relief representing the Holy Face. Below it is the marble statue of St. Veronica, fifteen feet high, holding the Holy Face in her hands.[16]

From time-to-time copies of the Holy Face on Veronica's Veil were made. In the sixteenth century, Jean de Dumex was the official painter at the court of Rome who was charged with the duty of distributing these "Veronicas" through-out the Christian world.[17] However during a long period (after the 1500s) it was forbidden, under pain of excommunication, to reproduce copies of the holy Effigy.[18]

---

[16] The Devotion to The Holy Face, JANVIER, p. 50

[17] The Devotion to The Holy Face, JANVIER, p. 47

[18] The Devotion to The Holy Face, JANVIER, p. 48

2 SISTER MARY OF ST. PETER (SR. MARIE ST. PIERRE) 1839 – Enters Carmel

1816 – 1848

Sr. Mary of St. Peter was born October 4, 1816, baptized in the church of St. Germain in the city of Rennes, France, and given the name Perrine Frances.

At her baptism she was given the same patrons as her father and mother -- St. Peter, Prince of the Apostles, and St. Francis of Assisi. Her father, Pierre Elnere, was a locksmith by profession. He married Francoise Portier, who bore him twelve children. This couple were fervent Christians. The Father daily assisted at mass, every evening visited the Blessed Sacrament, and during the day still found time to pray. Early on, he taught his little daughter the practice of the Way of the Cross, and her mother instilled in her a tender devotion to the Blessed Virgin.[19]

---

[19] Sister St. Pierre and the Work of Reparation, A Brief History, by Rev. Pierre Desire' Janvier, Director of the Priests of the Holy Face at Tours, translated by Mary Hoffman, published for the benefit of the Discalced Carmelites of New Orleans, 1885, p. 19-20

At twelve years of age, she lost her mother. Like St. Teresa, at the same age and under similar circumstances, she ran in her wild grief to Mary, threw herself at her feet, and implored her to be a mother to her in the place of the one that had been taken from her. The Queen of Heaven adopted this innocent soul and gave her through all her life sensible proofs of her maternal care.[20]

After losing her mother, her father labored assiduously to be able to bring up his children, and provide for them in their sickness which, for the most part, was long and fatal; for he beheld them all, one after the other consigned to the tomb, with the exception of one son and one daughter, who survived him. His glory before God and man was to have given to Carmel and to the Church his daughter of benediction.[21]

Perrine left Rennes for Tours to enter Carmel. Sr. Mary of St. Peter writes, "Accompanied by my father, I left the town of Rennes on the feast of my dear patron, St. Martin of Tours, the 11th of November 1839, and travelled towards Tourraine, my future home. I reached Tours on the 13th and proceeded immediately to the convent where I arrived at 5 o'clock in the afternoon. What rendered this event remarkable to me was, that it was St. Martin who presented me to 'all the saints of Carmel,' for on the next day their feast was to be celebrated. I felt assured that

---

[20] Sister St. Pierre and the Work of Reparation, 1885, p. 22

[21] Life of Sister Mary St. Peter Carmelite of Tours, written by herself, Arranged and Completed with the Aid of Her Letters and the Annals of Her Monastery, by M. L'abbe' Janvier, Director of the Priests of the Holy Face, 1884, p. 2

these good saints would not refuse me admission on the day of their feast, for I had prayed fervently, entreating them to admit me into their company; they could not have given me a better or more striking proof of my perseverance than that of having received me on such a day."[22]

"Shortly after entering the religious life, the God of mercy communicated Himself to my soul and made me understand for what purpose He had called me to Carmel…" Sister Mary continues, "Until now all of the communications which I had received from our Lord had but one end and that was the sanctification of my soul. Therefore, until now I had worked only for myself, being charged with the task of pursuing my own spiritual perfection. However, upon entering Carmel which is devoted to the needs of the Church, the glory of God and the salvation of souls, our Lord now inspired me with the spirit of sacrifice and zeal for the salvation of souls. This was, indeed, sublime virtue and unselfishness, but until then I knew nothing of them. Our Lord now communicated Himself to me on this subject, asking me to make an act of complete self-sacrifice to God for the accomplishment of His designs. This first call of our Lord in which He asked me to offer myself in self-surrender, I still consider as the very basis and foundation of the

---

[22] Life of Sister Mary St. Peter Carmelite of Tours, 1884, p. 58

Devotion of Reparation to His Holy Face, which He was later to reveal to me."[23]

From when she first arrived, her companions recognized in her a solid judgement united with a cheerful, equable disposition; she was reserved and very discreet; she shunned all self-seeking and singularity; her modesty, mortification, and obedience were most exemplary. The candor and tranquility of her face mirrored the innocence and serenity of her soul.[24]

Over a four-and-a-half-year period from 1843 - 1847, our Lord spoke to Sr. Mary of St. Peter revealing His desires for the work of Reparation and the Holy Face devotion. In obedience, Sr. Mary wrote down each communication she received from our Lord in detail as directed from her prioress, Mother Marie of the Incarnation. The following is a collection of several, although not all, of the Revelations our Lord gave to Sr. Mary which she wrote in detail in her autobiography.

[23] The Golden Arrow, the Autobiography and Revelations of Sister Mary of St. Peter on Devotion to the Holy Face, edited by Dorothy Scallan, St. Jerome Library Press, 2019, p. 49

[24] Sister Saint-Pierre and the Work of Reparation, 1885, p. 27

*Find the entire detailed collection of Sr. Mary's Revelations
in her autobiography entitled "the Golden Arrow"*

REVELATION of AUGUST 26, 1843
The Golden Arrow Prayer

("The Golden Arrow" page 112)

Our Lord opened His Heart to me and said: *"My Name is everywhere blasphemed! There are even children who blaspheme!"* He made me see that this frightful sin wounds His Divine Heart more grievously than all other sins, showing me how by blasphemy the sinner curses Him to His Face, attacks Him publicly, nullifies His redemption, and pronounces his own judgement and condemnation.

Our Lord then made me visualize the act of blasphemy as a poisoned arrow continually wounding His Divine Heart. After that He revealed to me that He wanted to give me a "Golden Arrow" which would have the power of wounding Him delightfully, and which would also heal these other wounds inflicted by the malice of sinners. The following is the formula of the "Golden Arrow" which is an Act of Praise that our Lord Himself dictated to me, notwithstanding my unworthiness, for the reparation of blasphemy against His Holy Name."[25]

---

[25] The Golden Arrow, p. 112-113

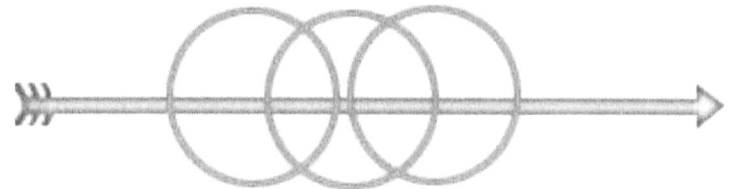

"THE GOLDEN ARROW"

May the most holy, most sacred, most adorable,
most incomprehensible, and unutterable Name of God,
be always praised, blessed, loved, adored, and glorified,
in heaven, on earth, and in the hells,
by all the creatures of God,
and by the Sacred Heart of our Lord Jesus Christ
in the most Holy Sacrament of the Altar.
Amen

Since I felt somewhat astonished at the words which our Lord used when He said to me, "in the hells," He made me understand that His Justice was also glorified there. I furthermore beg that notice be taken of this that our Lord did not say to me "in hell" (*dans l'enfer*), but He said, "in the hells" (*dans les enfers*), which can be understood to include also purgatory where He is loved and glorified by His suffering souls.[26]

---

[26] The Golden Arrow, p. 113

REVELATION of APPROXIMATELY NOVEMBER 15, 1843
The Chaplet of Reparation

("The Golden Arrow" page 124)

Our Lord inspired me at this time to compose certain prayers of reparation in the form of a Chaplet, or a small rosary. This Chaplet is made up of 33 small beads, on which is recited thirty-three times the prayer, "Arise Oh Lord, and let Your enemies be scattered, and let those that hate You flee before Your Face," and also six large [single] beads on which are recited the ejaculation, "My Jesus, mercy," followed by the doxology, "Glory Be to the Father, etc."

One day after Holy Mass our Lord appeared to me presenting me with a similar Chaplet which I saw was made of precious stones strung on a fine gold chain. Deeming myself quite unworthy of possessing such a treasure, I begged the Blessed Virgin to keep this beautiful rosary for me by placing it in her Immaculate Heart, and I also begged our Lord to attach indulgences to the recitation of this Chaplet.[27]

To pray the Chaplet, see page 115 of this book

---

[27] The Golden Arrow, p. 124

REVELATION of APPROXIMATELY
NOVEMBER 18, 1843
The Name of God will triumph

("The Golden Arrow" page 125)

One day during prayer, our Lord warned me in advance about the fury of Satan against this holy devotion, but He also consoled me saying: *"I give you My Name to be your light in the darkness and your strength in battle. Satan will do all in his power to crush this work at its roots. But I assure you that the Holy Name of God will triumph, and it will be the Holy Angels who will gain the victory in the conflict."*[28]

REVELATION of APPROXIMATELY
NOVEMBER 24, 1843
Our Lord urgently desires that there be formed an Association properly approved and well organized.

("The Golden Arrow" page 129)

Our Lord seized possession of the power of my soul and made me hear the following words: *"The whole earth is covered with crimes and the violation of the first three of the Ten Commandments of God has aroused the anger of My Father. The crimes that fill up the cup of wickedness are blasphemies against God's Holy Name and the profanation of Sundays.   These sins have reached to the very throne of*

---

[28] The Golden Arrow, p. 125

Almighty God, and they have provoked His wrath which is about to strike everywhere unless His Justice be appeased. Never before have these crimes reached such a peak." After that our Lord said:

"I desire, and this most urgently, that there be formed to honor the Name of My Father an Association, properly approved and well organized. Your superiors have good reasons to take only such steps in this devotion which are well founded, for otherwise My designs would not be fulfilled..."[29]

Then our Lord made me hear clearly that it was His desire to bestow mercy upon sinners by instituting this Work of Reparation. And as a parting remark He said to me: *"Oh, to whom shall I address myself if not to a Carmelite whose very vocation obliges her unceasingly to glorify My Name?"*[30]

REVELATION of FEBRUARY 2, 1844
The required daily prayers to practice
the devotion of Reparation.

("The Golden Arrow" page 133)

Our Lord told me that the Confraternity of Reparation which He desired to have established was to have a two-fold purpose, the first being Reparation for blasphemy, and the second being Reparation for the profanation of

---

[29] The Golden Arrow, p. 129-130

[30] The Golden Arrow, p. 130

Sunday, since these were the two principal sins which in modern times were provoking the anger of God.[31]

Our Savior also desires that the Association be placed under the patronage of St. Michael, St. Martin, and of St Louis, asking that each member should say daily one Our Father, one Hail Mary, and one Glory Be, together with the Act of Praise, called the Golden Arrow, which the Savior had previously dictated to me. But on Sunday and on feast days, all the Prayers of Reparation are to be recited, in order to make fitting reparation for the crimes committed against God's Majesty on these days of the Lord in order to obtain mercy for the guilty.[32]

Finally, our Lord told me that He desired each member of the Association to wear a special cross, and that on one side of this cross should be engraved the words, "Blessed be the Name of God, and on the reverse side should be the words, "Begone, Satan!" To all those wearing this holy cross our Lord promised a special resourcefulness to conquer the demon of blasphemy, adding that every time one hears a curse, he should repeat the two short inscriptions written on each side of the cross, and he will thus overcome the evil one and render glory to God.

At the end our Lord warned me, saying that the demon would do everything in his power to crush this Work which springs from the Sacred Heart[33]

---

[31] The Golden Arrow, p. 134

[32] The Golden Arrow, p. 134

[33] The Golden Arrow, p. 133-134

28

REVELATION of MARCH 16, 1844
The abomination of the sin of blasphemy

("The Golden Arrow" page 141)

During Holy Mass our Lord showed me the enormity of the crime of blasphemy, saying to me: *"You cannot comprehend the malice and abomination of this sin. If My Justice were not restrained by My Mercy, indeed, it would instantly crush the guilty..."*

After saying this, our Lord made me understand the excellence of the Work of Reparation and He made me see how the Devotion of Reparation surpasses other devotions, how pleasing it is to God as also to the Angels and Saints, and how beautiful it is to the Church.[34]

"Oh, if you only knew what great merit you acquire by saying even once, 'Admirable is the Name of God.' in the spirit of reparation for blasphemy!"[35]

---

[34] The Golden Arrow, p. 141

[35] The Golden Arrow, p. 142

REVELATION of OCTOBER 11, 1845
By practicing Reparation, we render our Lord the same service as did the pious Veronica

("The Golden Arrow" page 151)

Our Lord carried me in spirit to the road leading up to Calvary, and there He vividly showed me the pious deed of charity which St. Veronica performed toward Him when with her veil she wiped His Most Holy Face covered with spittle, dust, sweat, and blood.[36]

Following this, our Lord told me that by practicing Reparation for blasphemy, we render Him the same service as did the pious Veronica and that just as He looked with kindly eyes upon this holy woman during His Passion, so would He regard with affection all those who make reparation.[37]

---

[36] The Golden Arrow, p. 152-153

[37] The Golden Arrow, p. 153

REVELATION of OCTOBER 27, 1845
Our Lord seeks Veronicas to venerate His Divine Face

("The Golden Arrow" page 155)

I understood by this illumination that as the Sacred Heart of Jesus is the exterior object offered for our adoration to represent His boundless love in the most Holy Sacrament of the Altar, so in a parallel manner, in the Work of Reparation, the adorable Face of our Lord is the exterior object offered for the adoration of the members. I saw that by thus honoring and venerating this Sacred Countenance covered anew with outrages, we could atone for blasphemers who attack the Divinity of which this Holy Face is the figure, the mirror and the expression. By virtue of this Holy Face, offered to the Eternal Father, we can appease His anger, and obtain the conversion of the wicked and of blasphemers.[38]

Our Lord said to me: *"I seek Veronicas to wipe and venerate My Divine Face which has but few adorers!"* And then He reassured me that all persons who would apply themselves to this Work of Reparation would perform the same service in His behalf as that which the saintly Veronica had performed.[39]

He then added, *"By My Holy Face you will work wonders!"* Our Lord then declared that the gift of His Adorable Countenance which He presented to me on that

---

[38] The Golden Arrow, p. 156-157

[39] The Golden Arrow, p. 157

day was, next to the Sacraments, the greatest gift He could bestow on me.[40]

I was further given to understand that He had appointed St. Louis the protector of this Work of Reparation, and that St. Veronica was to be its protectress because of the service of love which she had rendered Him in wiping His adorable Face on the road to Calvary.[41]

REVELATION of OCTOBER 28, 1845

Bearing the picture of His Face,
One can purchase all he desires from God.

("The Golden Arrow" page 160)

Our Lord said, *"Just as in an earthly kingdom, money which is stamped with the picture of the sovereign or ruling executive of the country procures whatever one desires to purchase, so likewise in the Kingdom of Heaven, you shall obtain all that you desire by offering the coin of My precious Humanity which is My Adorable Face."*[42]

VRAIE IMAGE DE LA SAINTE FACE

---

[40] The Golden Arrow, p. 158

[41] The Golden Arrow, p. 158

[42] The Golden Arrow, p. 161

REVELATION OF NOVEMBER 5, 1845
His Sacred Face is like a Divine Stamp,
reproducing the Image of God in souls.

("The Golden Arrow" page 163)

By a divine illumination I see that this adorable Face is a Divine Stamp which has the power of imprinting anew the Image of God upon those souls to whom this Seal is applied. Transported with joy at this celestial vision I am moved, therefore, to salute the Holy Face in these words:

"I salute You, I adore You, and I love you, Oh adorable Face of my beloved Jesus, as the noble stamp of the Divinity! Completely surrendering my soul to you, I most humbly beg that this Seal be affixed upon us all so that the image of God may once more be reproduced by its imprint in our souls!"[43]

REVELATION of JANUARY 23, 1846
In order to obtain mercy, we must offer
the Eternal Father the Face of His Son.

("The Golden Arrow" page 168)

Our Lord said, *"The Face of this nation has become unsightly in the Eyes of My Father. The people are provoking the arm of His justice. To obtain mercy, offer therefore to the Eternal Father the Face of His Son in which He takes His delights. Unless this be done, the nation will experience God's*

---

[43] The Golden Arrow, p. 163

just punishments. Yet the country's deliverance from these evils lies in the Face of the Savior..." [44]

REVELATION of MARCH 12, 1846
Priests must openly from the pulpit preach and defend our Lord's cause of Reparation.

("The Golden Arrow" page 171)

Our Lord told me that the Good Thief (St. Dysmas) who so openly and boldly defended the Savior's cause on Calvary, is held up more especially as a model to priests who must now imitate him, and through their public preaching defend the cause of Reparation.[45]

Then our Lord promised me that all who defended His cause in the Work of Reparation, whether by their words, their prayers, or by their writings, He would Himself defend before His Eternal Father, and that He would give them His Kingdom. Our Lord urged me to extend this promise in His Name to His Priests, who through a crusade of preaching would advance the cause of Reparation.[46]

---

[44] The Golden Arrow, p. 168

[45] The Golden Arrow, p. 171-172

[46] The Golden Arrow, p. 172

REVELATION of MARCH 23, 1846
Our Lord desires to see this Work of Reparation built upon a solid foundation.

("The Golden Arrow" page 173)

Our Lord said, *"Do not be astonished at these promises which I make in favor of those who devote themselves to repairing for blasphemies against God's Holy Name through the Devotion to My Sacred Face because this Work of Reparation is the very essence of Charity, and those who possess Charity possess life"*[47]

He then said that it was He Himself, and His Spouse, Holy Church, who had given birth to this work of Reparation. But in order that this newly born Devotion should live and be properly received by the faithful, it must be established by the Divine Authority of our Holy Church. Our Lord desires to see this Work of Reparation built upon a solid foundation, and He said that its purpose, as well as all its precious advantages, must be known far and wide.[48]

---

[47] The Golden Arrow, p. 173

[48] The Golden Arrow, p. 173-174

THE MIRACLE AT LASALETTE - SEPTEMBER 19, 1846
Our Blessed Mother answers Sr. Mary's prayers

Our Lord revealed new lights to the Carmelite about the Work of Reparation, and they were reported to Archbishop Morlot, but there the matter rested. Sr. Marie Pierre wrote her reactions: "Since His Grace was unwilling to come to a decision in favor of the Work of the Reparation, I could well see that my only hope lay in prayer through the intercession of Mary, our powerful Advocate. Daily I recited the Rosary to obtain the establishment of the Reparation… 'O Holy Virgin, appear to someone in the world and reveal there the afflicting knowledge imparted to me!' "[49]

Great indeed was the surprise of the prioress when two months later, M. Leo Dupont (a faithful servant of God) came to the monastery with news of an incident about which everyone was commenting. "I have a reliable account of a wonderful apparition of Our Blessed Mother to two small children in the Alpine mountains at LaSalette. To these small children the Blessed Virgin addressed herself saying, *'If my people do not return to God by penance, I shall be forced to let fall the hand of My Son, because of the utter contempt for God's Commandments,*

---

[49] God Demands Reparation, The Holy Man of Tours, the Life of Leo Dupont, by Dorothy Scallan, St. Jerome Library Press, 2021, p. 130

especially the profanation of the Lord's Day and the crime of blasphemy.' "[50]

Here was the sign! Sr. Mary of St. Peter, who had enlisted the help of Mary to bring about the establishment of the Work of Reparation, promptly received her answer. Through Mary's intercession, two children on a mountainside were now proclaiming the same message which Sr. Mary had been repeating inside the cloister for more than two years! The need of Reparation for the crimes against God.[51]

It seemed an opportune time to press forward. The prioress, Leo Dupont, and a small group of interested persons decided to work toward having an account of Sr. Mary's communications disseminated under the title *'An Abridgement of Facts Concerning the Establishment of the Work of Reparation for Blasphemy.'*

This pamphlet in manuscript form was submitted to the Archbishop who approved it... However, wishing to conceal the name of Sr. Mary, who was still living, and the convent where the revelations took place, it was

---

[50] God Demands Reparation, p. 130-131

[51] God Demands Reparation, p. 131

agreed at first to issue only fifty copies of the *Abridgement of Facts*, and these not printed but written by hand…[52]

The contents of the small booklet excited the annoyance and disdain of certain individuals in politics. The matter was promptly brought to the attention of the diocesan authorities. The worst possible turn took place. The chancery office at once wrote the prioress, saying that the matter had been carried far beyond the Archbishop's intention. Complete silence was imposed on the Carmelite Monastery and on Leo Dupont…[53]

REVELATION of OCTOBER 25, 1846
God's excessive Mercy.
("The Golden Arrow" page 178)

The Divine Savior told me that in His excessive mercy He had given me His Heart as a Vase which alone was worthy of being presented to His Eternal Father to receive the bitter wine of His anger. Then He showed me that by passing through this Holy Channel, the bitter wine of God's anger would be changed for us into the sweet wine of His Mercy. The following is a prayer that our Lord dictated to me:

---

[52] God Demands Reparation, p. 131-132

[53] God Demands Reparation, p. 132

*"Eternal Father, look upon
the Sacred Heart of Jesus which
I offer to You as a Vase
that it might receive
the wine of Your Justice,
and in passing through
this Holy Channel
that it may be changed for us
into the Wine of Your Mercy!"
Amen.* [54]

REVELATION of NOVEMBER 22, 1846
Through this Holy Face
you will obtain the conversion of sinners.

("The Golden Arrow" page 182)

Our Lord told me, "*...The treasure of My Holy Face in itself possesses such tremendous value that through It all the affairs of My household can readily be settled. Through this Holy Face you will obtain the conversion of many sinners. Nothing that you ask in virtue of the Holy Face will be refused you. Oh, if you only knew how pleasing is the sight of My Face to My Father!*" [55]

---

[54] The Golden Arrow, p. 179

[55] The Golden Arrow, p. 182

For two years, the Carmelites were forced to leave their monastery and live in a secular dwelling where cloister enclosure that they practiced was barely possible. In spite this, Sr. Mary con-  tinued to fulfil her duties as Portress and suffered a great deal with distractions and embarrassments. However, our Lord consoled her with new insights.

In her great desire to comfort and strengthen those who came to her with their sorrows, she was inspired to communicate to them the devotion of the Gospel of the Circumcision, and of the Holy Name. Thus, she writes on this devotion: "The demon uses all possible means to snatch from our Lord Jesus Christ the inheritance purchased by the Cross, and is ever seeking to rob this Good Shepherd of the lambs obtained at so great a price. To put this ravishing wolf to flight, Jesus has made known to me that He wishes His sheep marked with His Holy Name, by bearing on their person the Gospel which announces to all nations that the Incarnate Word was named Jesus. This amiable Savior has acquainted me with the virtue of His Sacred Name -- that it would drive away the demon, and that all those placing themselves under its special protection would receive great graces." Her superiors permitted her to distribute printed sheets of this Gospel on which was stamped an image of the Infant Jesus... These sheets were folded and enclosed in a little square sachet. On the sheets, beneath the Gospel, these words were inscribed: "When Jesus was named, Satan, vanquished, was disarmed."[56]

"Our Lord revealed to me," said the Sister, "how glorious it is to Him to have His victory celebrated by these words, for they make the demon tremble with rage; that He will bless all who wear this Gospel, and will defend them against the attacks of Satan."[57]

In honor of the five letters which form the name of Jesus, and in virtue of His five wounds, He promised to grant five special graces to all who would practice this devotion.

1st - To preserve them from death by lightning.

2nd - To protect them from the snares and malice of the devil.

3rd - To deliver them from a sudden and unprovided death.

4th - To assist them to advance with facility in the path of virtue.

5th - That He would give them the grace of final perseverance.[58]

---

[56] The Manual of the Holy Face, A.M.P., Seventh Part – The Life of Sister Marie de St. Pierre, St. Paul Press, 2018, p. 356

[57] The Manual of the Holy Face, A.M.P., p. 357

[58] Life of Sister Mary St. Peter Carmelite of Tours, 1884, p. 221

Sister Mary writes, "The means of covering these expenses, my Divine Master directed me to address myself to His servant, M. Leo Dupont, and to say to him, that the Infant Jesus requested of him this work of charity as the tithe of all the benefits He had bestowed upon him.[59]

We read in his life, that this fervent layman, aided the virgin of Carmel to pursue her cherished devotions. Before the little gospels had been printed, he himself, copied them, and assisted to distribute them among the faithful.[60]

[59] Life of Sister Mary St. Peter Carmelite of Tours, 1884, p. 222

[60] Life of Sister Mary St. Peter Carmelite of Tours, 1884, p. 222

REVELATION of JANUARY 21, 1847
The Name of God and the Holy Face are inseparable.

("The Golden Arrow" page 187)

Our Savior complained that His love in the Most Blessed Sacrament of the Altar was not appreciated because of the lack of faith among Christians...

Yes, it is through this august Sacrament that Jesus, our Savior, desires to impart to souls the rare virtue emanating from His most Holy Face, for indeed there in the Blessed Sacrament of the Altar His adorable Face is more dazzling than the sun...[61]

Because the most Holy Name of God expresses the Divinity, and all the perfections of the Creator, it follows from this that blasphemers of this Sacred Name attack God Himself. Recalling the words of our Lord Who said, *"I am in the Father and the Father is in Me,"* we must realize that since Jesus through His Incarnation became capable of suffering, it is He who endures in His Adorable Face the insults offered to the Name of God, His Father, by blasphemers. The impious, through their blasphemies attack His Adorable Face, and that the Faithful glorify this Holy Face by the praises they confer on the Holy Name of God.[62]

---

[61] The Golden Arrow, p. 187

[62] The Golden Arrow, p. 188

REVELATION of MARCH 7, 1847
The Work of Reparation to the Holy Face is "the most beautiful work under the sun."

("The Golden Arrow" page 196)

I have great confidence that this Work will be established because our Lord Himself assured me of this. For that reason, therefore I would never abandon my hope in Him who is Omnipotent, even though I saw both the earth and hell itself opposing this work...

Our Lord gave me the following promise saying: *"Rejoice, my daughter, because the hour approaches when the most beautiful work under the sun will be born. Offer My Sacred Heart to the Eternal Father to obtain it."*[63]

---

[63] The Golden Arrow, p. 196

REVELATION of APRIL 6, 1847
Sr. Mary is encouraged by our Lord
to continue her valiant battle against Communism.

("The Golden Arrow" page 206)

Our Lord has given me the grace to launch an offensive warfare.

I begin by placing my soul in our Lord's hands… After doing this I proceed to enter the battlefield, fortified with the Cross and the other Instruments of our Lord's tortures as my weapons of war… Then I say:

"May God arise and let His enemies be scattered, and let all those who hate Him flee before His Face!

"May the thrice Holy Name of God overthrow all their plans!"

"May the Holy Name of the Living God split them up by disagreements!

"May the terrible Name of God of Eternity stamp out all their godlessness!

"Lord, I do not desire the death of the sinner, but I want him to be converted and to live. 'Father, forgive them for they know not what they do.'"

Feeling disturbed about uttering these imprecations, I sometimes worry but I must make it clear that never do I have the intention to wish evil to the enemy. I desire only to oppose their wickedness and their passions. In short, what I want is to kill not them, but the "evil spirit" within them.[64]

---

[64] The Golden Arrow, p. 206-207

SR. MARY OF ST. PETER'S DEATH
SHE DIED IN THE ODOR OF SANCTI TY JULY 8, 1848

On March 30, 1848, shining with glory, our Lord appeared to the faithful apostle of His work of Reparation and said:

"You are near the goal of your earthly pilgrimage. The end of the combat approaches. You will soon behold My Face in Heaven..."[65]

Although Sister Mary was until now apparently in fair health, following all the religious exercises prescribed by the Holy Rule, and performing all her duties as Portress Sister, she suddenly developed certain alarming symptoms and was found to be mortally ill with severe pulmonary tuberculosis.[66]

Shortly before she died, she was asked about the Devotion to the Holy Face, to which she answered:

"I have the greatest hopes. The plans of the wicked will be foiled! It was to accomplish this that the Work of Reparation to the Holy Face was revealed. Now that this is done, my career ended for it was for this Work that God had placed me on earth, as our Lord has made known to me. Oh, how true it is that God has means of satisfying His justice which are unknown to men."[67]

---

[65] The Golden Arrow, p. 219

[66] The Golden Arrow, p. 220

[67] The Golden Arrow, p. 220

Sr. Mary of St. Peter died in the odor of sanctity on July 8, 1848, at the age of thirty-three.

After her death, the Archbishop of Tours, had placed an interdict on the Carmelite's writings. All the revelations which she had received in life and which she had written down in her own hand were gathered together, formally sealed by the Archbishop personally, and then locked up in the diocesan archives. Nothing was allowed either to be written or spoken in connection with Sr. Mary of St. Peter's mission.[68]

---

[68] God Demands Reparation, p. 144

Vatican Late 19th Century

Saint Peter's Basilica Mid to Late 19th Century

In January of 1849, six months after the death of Sr. Mary of St. Peter, the Holy Father Pius IX from his exile in Gaeta, ordered public prayers to be offered in all the churches of Rome to implore God's mercy on the pontifical states. Revolutionary disorders were shaking not only Catholic France but the eternal city of Rome, itself. [69]

---

[69] God Demands Reparation, p. 145

Complying with the Pope's orders for special public prayers in Rome, a three-day exposition of the True Wood of the Cross and the Relic of Veronica's Veil was held for public veneration at St. Peter's Basilica. And it was here that an unusual prodigy took place, for on the third day of the exposition, a miracle occurred in connection with the Sacred Veil. The Cannons appointed to guard the precious relics during the exhibition, and also some of the faithful who knelt in St. Peter's Basilica, noticed a remarkable change on the Veil of the Holy Face, the impression of which was so faint as to be scarcely visible[70]

Through another veil of silk which covers the true Relic of Veronica's Veil, and absolutely prevents the features from being distinguished, the Divine Face appeared distinctly, as if living, and was illumined by a soft light; the features assumed a death-like hue, and the eyes, deep-sunken, wore an expression of great pain. The Cannons immediately notified the clergy; the people were called in [by the ringing of the Basilica bells]. Many wept; all were impressed with a reverential awe. An apostolic notary was summoned; a certificate was drawn up attesting the fact. A copy of it was sent to the Holy Father at Gaeta. For many days this prodigy, which lasted three hours, was the sole topic of conversation at Rome.[71]

Soon afterward, copies of the true Image of the Holy Face were printed on Holy Linen and later sent abroad.

---

[70] God Demands Reparation, p. 145

[71] God Demands Reparation, p. 145-146

The certificates of authenticity that accompanied the images verified that the images were touched to the three instruments of our Lord's Passion. They were each touched to Veronica's Veil, the True Wood of the Cross, and the Lance that pierced Christ's side.

Several of these true copies of the Holy Face reached the Prioress of the Benedictines at Arras, who, acquainted with the revelations of Sr. Marie Pierre concerning Devotion to the Holy Face, promptly sent some of them to the Carmelite sisters at Tours.[72]

VERA EFFIGIES SACRI VULTUS DOMINI NOSTRI IESU CHRISTI

The Vatican continued the practice of making copies of the Holy Face of Jesus on holy linen until the early 1900s. Each image being touched to the three instruments of our Lord's Passion and sent out into the world for veneration. It is not known how many images were made over the approximate seventy-year period.

These images, having been touched to the blood of Christ through the instruments of our Lord's Passion, are placed in a relic class of their very own. They are considered "Living Images of

---

[72] God Demands Reparation, p. 146

Jesus Christ". *The copies which are painted on linen or silk, if they are furnished with a seal of authentication, enjoy the same privileges as the miraculous picture (Veronica's Veil) itself, and, according to the rules of the liturgy, ought to be equally honored; therefore, it is not proper to expose them to public veneration unless a lamp or a taper be kept constantly burning before them.*[73]

Children of God, look on the divine Face of your Savior, weeping, suffering, expiring through grief and

love of you! At the sight of it let your hard hearts be softened and touched with compassion. Present It to the heavenly Father, saying with the accents of faith and the humility of a contrite heart-- *"Oh God, our Protector, behold the state to which we are reduced, look at the Face of Thy Christ, and save us."*[74]

---

[73] Manual of the Archconfraternity of the Holy Face, Rev. Abbe Janvier, Priest of the Holy Face, Translated by Mrs. A.R. Bennett, Tours, the Oratory of the Holy Face, 1887, p. 79-80

[74] The Devotion to the Holy Face, JANVIER, p. 57

Leo Papin-Dupont, the devout servant of the Holy Face and of St. Martin, was born January 27, 1797, in Martinique. His father, Nicolas Leon Papin-Dupont, the descendant of a noble family of Brittany... His mother was Marie Louise Gaigneron de Marolles who, in a few years, was left a widow with two

children, Leon, and Theobald… Leon's childhood passed under the guardianship of his mother… who instilled into her son a veneration for the great truths of faith, and a love for the service of God.[75]

Leon made his first communion at the age of twelve. We know that Mr. Dupont always regarded this grace as the greatest he had received during his life, and he would often say that his soul had been then inundated with a

---

[75] The Holy Man of Tours, or, the Life of Leon Papin-Dupont, who Died at Tours in the Odor of Sanctity, March 18, 1876, Pierre Desire Janvier 1882, p. 1

heavenly joy. In this Sacrament, he derived that ardent and tender devotion for the holy Eucharist.[76]

At the age of nineteen, Leo departed to study in Paris as a student of law. Since the family wealth, to which Leo would fall heir, consisted of vast sugar plantations in Martinique, it was deemed advisable for Leo to pursue a course of studies that would launch him upon a lawyer's career, so that after his return he could fill some honorable post in the government of the French colony.[77]

Throughout his time in Paris, Leo continued to deeply feel his call to the priesthood. Two days after graduation, he visited the Sulpician Seminary. The priest who was interviewing him invited him to go to Notre Dame the next day to attend the ordination rites. As he observed the service, Leo's eyes remained fixed on the altar, absorbed in the holy drama.

Suddenly, something caught Leo's attention. Something the Bishop was doing made his blood run cold. He lost all rapture as he watched the bishop anointing the hands of each ordinand with holy chrism. First the thumb and index finger of each hand, then a cross on the palm. Leo needed no words to tell him what this meant. Slowly, he turned his eyes away from the sanctuary. Mechanically, he now unfolded his hands and stared at his own thumb, the stub of something which had once in childhood resembled a thumb -- but which was

---

[76] The Holy Man of Tours, Janvier, p.3

[77] God Demands Reparation, p. 8

now deformed...[78] The anointed hands of the priest were destined to hold the Body of Jesus Christ, True God and True Man, under the species of bread and wine. To be a priest, a man had to be whole. His hand was deformed. A freak accident in childhood had robbed him of his thumb,[79] and robbed him of the possibility of ever becoming a priest.

Leo returned to Martinique. That fall, he was offered a position as royal councilor at court.

One and one-half years later, on May 9th, 1827, Leo married Caroline 'd Audiffredi, who he had been acquainted with for many years. After five years they had a daughter and named her Henriette. Sadly, his wife Caroline, passed away when Henriette was only ten months old.

When Henriette was two and one-half years old, Leo, his mother (Madame Arnaud), and little Henriette, left Martinique and moved to Tours, France, in order to fulfill Caroline's wish that Henriette be brought up by the Ursuline Sisters as she had been raised herself.

Leo knew full well the importance of living one's life for God, and for God alone. After living in Tours for a few years, he continued to spend his days giving himself to God through prayer, good works, and penance.

To undo some of the harm spread by anti-Catholic writings, Leo decided to write a booklet on the

---

[78] God Demands Reparation, Scallan, p. 66-67

[79] God Demands Reparation, Scallan, p. 67

Eucharist... which required a great deal of research on his part. In addition, he consulted the Fathers of the Church and the Bible, with which he became well acquainted as a result of his practice of daily reciting the long Divine Office.[80]

When the booklet was completed, Leo published it anonymously under the title, *Faith Revived and Piety Reanimated Through the Eucharist.* He brought his first copies to the Carmelite Monastery.[81]

Leo felt a particular attraction to the Carmelites, whose life of prayer and solitude he sincerely admired. They, in turn, came to look on him not only as their benefactor, who by his frequent alms made it possible for them to continue their lives of retirement, but as a friend. Being strictly cloistered, the sisters needed someone on whom they could rely when there was something to be attended to in the outside world. And as the years went by, the prioress, Mother Mary of the Incarnation, found herself invariably turning to Leo to settle their business for them.[82]

But she had no inkling when Leo handed her his new publication, that in the not-so-distant future she would be calling on him to attend not only to some of their worldly business, but a work as unworldly as anything that had ever happened. The work would have to do with a new

---

[80] God Demands Reparation, Scallan, p. 116

[81] God Demands Reparation, Scallan, p. 116

[82] God Demands Reparation, Scallan, p. 116-117

postulant whom they had just admitted into the cloister, a young girl of twenty-three whose name, Sister Marie de St. Pierre, was destined to make history.[83]

After Sr. Mary of St. Peter began receiving the Revelations from our Savior, her prioress felt it necessary to consult with Leo Dupont on this matter and seek his help. From that point on, Leo devoted himself to working with Sr. Mary to accomplish God's designs concerning the Work of Reparation.

After three years had passed with abundant Revelations being given to Sr. Mary of St. Peter, she declared that the exterior emblem would be the outraged Face of Christ; and acting on this, she had composed the Litany of the Holy Face and other analogous prayers. A pamphlet was arranged which contained the substance of the divine communications, and which was called: "*Abridgement of the Facts Concerning the Work for the Reparation of Blasphemy.*" This pamphlet, intended for circulation among a few Carmelite houses and a small number of pious souls, was submitted in manuscript to the Archbishop, and was approved by him. Mr. Dupont, again placing his services at the disposal of the Carmelite Community, distributed these pamphlets among his friends.[84]

Leo Dupont had frequent interviews with Sister Saint Pierre. The fervent layman following with ever increasing

---

[83] God Demands Reparation, Scallan, p. 117

[84] The Holy Man of Tours, Janvier, p. 64-65

interest the action of God on this privileged soul... As Sr. Mary filled the office of portress, Mr. Dupont went frequently to receive her commissions and to recommend himself to her prayers. She presented him little cases containing the Gospel which is read on the Feast of the Circumcision. The pious Sister, to honor the divine Infant, had made numerous copies of this short Gospel and had enclosed them in little cases prepared for the purpose. Mr. Dupont assisted the Sister both in copying and distributing the Gospels.[85]

In 1847, Sr. Mary was given a complete series of revelations foretelling the great world upheaval known as Communism of which the cloistered nun at Carmel, knew nothing. That summer, a copy of "*Abridgement of Facts*" had come to the attention of Bishop Parisis, of the Diocese of Langres. So impressed was the prelate with the revelations of the Carmelite mystic that he decided to take steps to establish the Confraternity of Reparation in his own diocese… The Bishop at once dispatched one of his priests to Rome to ask the Holy Father, Pope Pius IX, to grant a Brief for the erection of a Confraternity of Reparation in the parish Church of St. Dizier, in the Diocese of Langres. The Holy Father willingly granted the requested Brief…[86]

Although the newly formed Confraternity at Langres was not the full project of Reparation outlined in the

---

[85] The Holy Man of Tours, Janvier, p. 66-67

[86] God Demands Reparation, Scallan, p. 135-136

revelations of St. Marie Pierre, it was a definite step forward, and Leo Dupont was heartened at hearing the news.

But Leo could not have known the tragedy that was about to strike his family. A contagious fever had struck Tours. The disease had reached the proportions of a raging epidemic. Schools were ordered closed, and Henriette, now fifteen, was sent home until the epidemic should relent.[87]

Although well and cheerful when she arrived home, Henriette became ill the following morning. On the third day, Leo appealed to Sr. Marie Pierre for prayers. She sent back word that although she had prayed earnestly, she could hold out no hope for Henriette's recovery. God seemed to demand this great sacrifice from Leo.[88] Henriette passed away quietly on the fourth day. Everything dear to Leo was being taken from him.[89]

The sorrow in Leo's heart at this last blow made him sever every last tie he might have had for this earth. Hereafter, he would live entirely for God, completely detached from everything. The large dowry he had reserved for Henriette he now turned over to charitable causes, among which were convents, churches, and orphanages. The largest share of his donations he

---

[87] God Demands Reparation, Scallan, p. 136

[88] God Demands Reparation, Scallan, p. 137

[89] God Demands Reparation, Scallan, p. 138

reserved for the Little Sisters of the Poor, and to fund a house for poor missionary priests.[90]

At the end of March 1848, Sister Marie Pierre became ill. She was diagnosed with pulmonary tuberculosis. Within three months she was reduced to a veritable skeleton.[91] She died in the odor of sanctity on July 8, 1848. Mr. Dupont assisted at the funeral obsequies and accompanied her mortal remains to the cemetery. From that time, he was accustomed to praying frequently at the tomb of the venerated Sister, and he took care that it should be kept in good order.[92]

Returning home from Sr. Marie Pierre's funeral, Leo wondered what would become of the Devotion to the Holy Face now that the Carmelite had died. Leo learned that the Archbishop of Tours had placed an interdict on the dead Carmelite's writings. They were sealed and locked up in the diocesan archives.[93]

After the Miracle of 1849 (see chapter 3), copies of the true Image of the Holy Face were printed, touched to the True Veil, and later sent abroad. Several of these true copies of the Holy Face reached the Prioress of the Benedictines at Arras, who, acquainted with the revelations of Sister Marie Pierre concerning Devotion to

_____

[90] God Demands Reparation, Scallan, p. 139

[91] God Demands Reparation, Scallan, p. 143

[92] The Holy Man of Tours, Janvier, p. 70-71

[93] God Demands Reparation, Scallan, p. 144

the Holy Face, promptly sent some of them to the Carmelite Sisters at Tours. The prioress of the Carmelites, Mother Mary of the Incarnation, at once sent two of these pictures of the Holy Face to Leo Dupont.[94]

Leo had the two pictures framed. He gave one to the members of the Society of Nocturnal Adoration, which he himself had founded two years previously, and the other he hung in his parlor.[95] He took it upon himself to burn an oil lamp next to the picture as a constant sign of veneration and love.

Two days after hanging the picture, on the morning of Holy Saturday, the first healing miracle took place in Leo's home. A woman came to discuss a business matter. He noticed that she was rubbing her eyes and seemed to be in great discomfort. When he asked her about it, she told him that her eyes gave her great pain. He suggested that she put some oil from the lamp on her eyes, then he knelt with her and prayed before the Holy Face. Her cure was instantaneous. The pain and discomfort immediately ceased.

Within several weeks, more than twenty persons had been relieved of serious illnesses. Leo went to the Carmelites and spoke to the prioress to let her know of the healing miracles taking place in his parlor.

By the end of the year, so many miraculous cures were obtained by anointing with the oil from the lamp and the

---

[94] God Demands Reparation, Scallan, p. 146

[95] God Demands Reparation, Scallan, p. 146

recitation of the Litany of the Holy Face, composed by Sister Marie Pierre, that Leo was unable to keep an exact count of them.[96]

It was three years now since Leo had begun his Devotion to the Holy Face by hanging in his parlor the Vera Effigies, and henceforth it was to fill his whole life. Taking a photograph of his picture of the Holy Face, he had 25,000 lithograph copies made and distributed at his own expense.[97]

In 1854, only three years since the first miraculous cure, approximately 60,000 bottles of the oil (from the lamp) had been given away. Requests for oil poured into Leo's home, not only from France, but from distant parts of Europe, and even from America...[98]

Despite all the healing miracles, Cardinal Morlot of Tours, had still not given his approval for the Work of Reparation. In 1855 Cardinal Morlot was appointed the new Archbishop of Paris, and Tours new ordinary was now Monsignor Guibert.

The years passed. Leo was now sixty-eight. He spent almost all his time in the parlor before the Image of the Holy Face. Visitors still came to his house... Requests for

---

[96] God Demands Reparation, Scallan, p. 149

[97] God Demands Reparation, Scallan, p. 150

[98] God Demands Reparation, Scallan, p. 150-151

pictures of the Holy Face and for vials of the holy oil continued unabated.[99]

Since 1851, Leo had distributed approximately one million vials of oil... Leo had invited the suffering into his parlor, knelt with them, prayed with them, and anointed their sores tirelessly during a span that had stretched now for fifteen years...[100] Hundreds of healing miracles had taken place in his parlor. He also had the burden of handling a tremendous amount of correspondence from all over the world... The Devotion to the Holy Face had become for him a full-time career.[101]

Leo Dupont died on March 18, 1876. He was declared Venerable by the Holy See during Pope Pius XII's Pontificate and has been awaiting beatification since 1939.

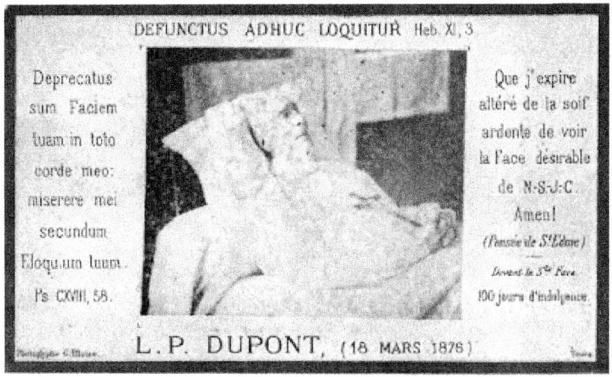

---

[99] God Demands Reparation, Scallan, p. 173

[100] God Demands Reparation, Scallan, p. 176

[101] God Demands Reparation, Scallan, p. 176

It is important to note that as the years passed, Archbishop Guibert was succeeded by Archbishop Fruchaud. Then, after the death of Cardinal Morlot, Archbishop Fruchaud was succeeded by Archbishop Colet.

THE ORATORY OF THE HOLY FACE
TOURS, FRANCE
1876 – Present

L'ORATOIRE AU 14 SEPTEMBRE 1877.
AU - DESSUS DE LA PORTE D'ENTRÉE : *Sanctissima Facies Christi Jesu.*

After Mr. Dupont's death, there was a natural desire to know what would become of the venerated picture of the Holy Face, which, for so many years had been the one object of his life, and which had been honored in his home by so many miracles... When making arrangements concerning his property, his confidence in God and his humble discretion had dictated to him the following

64

words: "That I do not speak of the Holy Face in my will, is not the result of forgetfulness. I do not wish to interfere in the question which may arise, when I shall no longer be there to maintain the lamps in my parlor. God will provide according to His holy will."[102]

One month after Leo's death, the house at 8 Rue St. Etienne was put up for sale… When news of the proposed sale reached the Carmelite Monastery, the Sisters decided to intervene. Although quite poor, they had recently been favored with a substantial contribution, and they now appealed to the Archbishop to use the sum to buy the famous house on the Rue St. Etienne. This proposal met with the Prelate's complete and prompt approval… Archbishop Colet offered to take formal steps to convert the private domicile of the Holy Man of Tours into a public oratory.[103] Workmen were at once hired… The parlor where the Picture of the Holy Face hung, and the room adjoining it, which was the dining hall, were made into one large room… This room was to be the Oratory. Here an altar was erected.[104]

Archbishop Colet formed a diocesan Society of Priests who were to reside in the holy house on Rue St. Etienne under a rule, with the purpose of dedicating their lives to the spread of the Cult of the Holy Face. They were to be known as Priests of the Holy Face. From this Oratory,

---

[102] The Holy Man of Tours, Janvier, p. 470

[103] God Demands Reparation, Scallan, p. 202

[104] God Demands Reparation, Scallan, p. 203

pamphlets and booklets bearing his "imprimatur" were to be disseminated throughout the diocese…[105]

The Archbishop installed Father Peter Janvier as the first director of the new community… (Fr. Janvier knew Leo for many years and was a dear friend). He also instructed Fr. Janvier to begin collating facts and data on the two adorers of the Holy Face, with the intention of publishing two full-length biographies, one the Life of Sister Marie Pierre, and the other the Life of the venerable Leo Dupont.[106] After these books were published, the Holy Face Devotion began to spread far and wide throughout Europe, and then America.

Archbishop Colet, noting the admirable response of the Catholic Faithful to the Work of Reparation, now felt the hour had come for him to appeal to the Pope for the Brief which would validly perpetuate the Work of the Holy Face until the end of time.[107]

But before he could do this, Archbishop Colet became ill. After a brief sickness, he passed away quietly.

A few months later, Archbishop William Meignan was installed as the new Bishop of Tours… The new Archbishop did not leave the faithful of his diocese in doubt as to his intentions concerning the Holy Face Devotion. He soon issued an Ordinance establishing The Confraternity of the Holy Face in the Oratory on the Rue

---

[105] God Demands Reparation, Scallan, p. 205

[106] God Demands Reparation, Scallan, p. 205

[107] God Demands Reparation, Scallan, p. 207

St. Etienne... The time was now ripe to petition the Holy See for a Brief that would raise the Confraternity of the Holy Face to the rank of Archconfraternity and thus insure its perpetuity.[108]

Nearly sixty bishops and archbishops from France, Belgium, Italy, Spain, Switzerland, Austria, England, Ireland, the United States, and Canada hastened to sign their names recommending the petition to Pope Leo XIII.[109]

According to the customs of the Court of Rome, the favor solicited in the petition could not be granted at once, but would have to come in degrees and in successive portions. For example, the power of attaching or aggregating would have to be granted first to the Diocese of Tours, later France, then some neighboring countries, until at last it would come to include the whole world.[110]

However, Pope Leo XIII bypassed these customs as he wrote, *"Non tam pro Gallia, quam ubique"*. Not only for all of France, but for the whole world! Rome had spoken. An irrevocable verdict had been pronounced.[111]

The official document entitled "Brief of His Holiness Pope Leo XIII, establishing The Archconfraternity of the

---

[108] God Demands Reparation, Scallan, p. 208

[109] God Demands Reparation, Scallan, p. 208

[110] God Demands Reparation, Scallan, p. 209

[111] God Demands Reparation, Scallan, p. 209

Holy Face," was forwarded to Tours. The mission of Sister Marie Pierre had been realized.[112]

Thousands of adorers from all over the world still visit the Holy Face Oratory. They come to worship our Savior, to venerate the Holy Face image, to visit the tomb of the Holy Man of Tours, and see the lamp that still continues to burn in veneration.

Leo Dupont's original Holy Face of Jesus image which still hangs in the Oratory of the Holy Face in Tours, France.

---

[112] God Demands Reparation, Scallan, p. 209

5   1885 THE ARCHCONFRATERNITY

OF THE HOLY FACE

An Archconfraternity, according to the organization of the Church, is possessed of great importance. Archconfraternities occupy the first rank, after the ecclesiastical hierarchy, the religious orders and the different institutions approved by the Holy See.[113]

By virtue of the Apostolic Brief, the devotion to the Holy Face and the practice of Reparation are *united* in our Archconfraternity; they *complete* each other, and are, as it were, fused into one another. Henceforward, the two works no longer run the risk of being separated from one another in the mind of the faithful.[114]

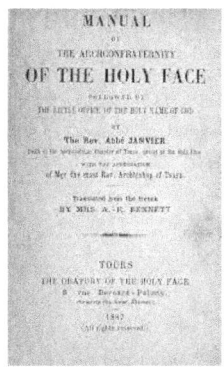

To this day, you may join the Archconfraternity of the Holy Face by sending a written request to the Oratory:

Centre Spirituel de la Sainte Face
8, rue Bernard Palissy,
37000 Tours, France

Email:
Recteur.oratoiresainteface@gmail.com

---

[113] The Manual of the Holy Face A.M.P., p. 35

[114] The Manual of the Holy Face A.M.P., p. 37

BRIEF OF HIS HOLINESS POPE LEO XIII

*ESTABLISHING THE ARCHCONFRATERNITY
OF THE HOLY FACE, OCTOBER 1, 1885*

Manual of the Archconfraternity of the Holy Face 1887, pgs. 23-26

Leo XIII Pope,
For a Perpetual remembrance

According to the usages of Roman Pontiffs, our predecessors, we are accustomed to decorate and enrich with special honors and privileges the pious associations instituted for the practice of works of piety and charity. Our well-beloved sons, directors and associates of the pious Confraternity known as that of the Holy Face, canonically established in the sanctuary of the same name, in the town of Tours, and enriched by us and the Holy See with numerous privileges, have expressed to us the desire, that making use of the plentitude of our apostolic power, we should honor this association with the title of Archconfraternity and with the preeminence which is its due.

Desirous of giving to each and all of those in whose favor these letters are delivered a special mark of our benevolence, and only as regards the present case, considering them as absolved, and to be absolved from all sentences of excommunication and interdict, and from all the censures and ecclesiastical penalties which they may have incurred and which may have been inflicted on them in any manner or for any cause whatsoever, we, by our apostolical authority, in virtue of these presents, establish and constitute as a perpetual Archconfraternity, with the accustomed privileges, the so called Confraternity of the Holy Face, established in the town of Tours. And by the same our authority, in virtue of these letters, we concede and grant in perpetuity, to the directors and colleagues present and future of the Archconfraternity, the power, validly and lawfully, to aggregate to itself, throughout the whole world, excepting in our glorious city, all the other Confraternities existing in the same name and having the same object, observing always the form prescribed by the Constitution of Pope Clement VIII, our predecessor of happy memory, and the other apostolical ordinances drawn up on this subject, as well as to communicate to all and each the Indulgences, remissions of sins and dispensations of penance, which have been granted by the Holy Apostolic See to the association so erected by us into an Archconfraternity, and which are susceptible of being communicated to others.

We decree that our present letters shall be, for the present and the future, fixed, valid and efficacious; that they shall obtain and possess their full and entire effects, that they shall fully favor all and for all, whom they concern and shall concern hereafter in accordance with what has been previously enumerated, and shall be judged and defined by ordinary judges and delegates, whoever they may be, even the auditors of the suits of the Apostolic Palace, the Nuncios of the Holy See, the Cardinals of the Holy Roman Church, even legates *a latere* and all other personages, whatever their dignity and their power may be; entire power authority to judge and interpret otherwise being withdrawn from them in general and in particular, so that if any one, whatever be the authority with which he is invested, attacks any of these clauses knowingly or through ignorance, his act shall be null and void.

And this notwithstanding the Constitutions and Apostolic ordinances, and, in as far as is necessary, the statutes, customs, and uses contrary to the above-named Confraternity and all others, even when they have been confirmed by apostolic oath or any other decision whatever.

Given at Rome, near St. Peter, under the ring of the fisherman, the 1st day of October 1885, being the eighth year of our Pontificate.

✝ Place of the Seal.

✝ Cardinal
Ledochowski
Examined,
We commend its execution
and its use.

GUILLAUME-RENE,
Archbishop of Tours.

✝ Place of the Seal.

Pope Leo XIII - 1887

72

STATUTES AND RULES OF THE ARCHCONFRATERNITY OF THE HOLY FACE

Manual of the Archconfraternity of the Holy Face 1887, pgs. 52-54

I.   The Archconfraternity of the Holy Face has, with the authority of the Holy See, been established at Tours in the chapel of the same name, where, since the year 1852, an authentic copy of St. Veronica's veil (preserved at Saint Peter's at Rome) has been specially venerated.

II. The chief object of this Archconfraternity is:

1. To offer to the adorable and suffering Face of our Lord Jesus Christ, imprinted on St. Veronica's veil, the homage of worship and love which is Its due.

2. To induce members, by honoring this Holy and venerable effigy, to perform acts of faith, piety, zeal and penance, in order to make reparation for the terrible outrages which, in these days of impiety, are constantly committed against the Majesty of God, the Divinity of our Lord and the authority of the Church.

III. Members undertake the following obligations:

1. To recite every day, for the intentions of the Archconfraternity, either in Latin or English, one *Pater, Ave, Gloria,* and the invocation: *Domine ostende Faciem tuam, et salvi erimus:*

73

"Lord, show us Thy Face, and we shall be saved".

2. To wear an effigy of the Holy Face, either on a cross, medal, or scapular.
3. To attend as often as possible the monthly meetings held in the chapel where the association is established.
4. To extend as much as they can the devotion to the suffering Face of our Savior.
5. To have their names entered on the register of the association.

IV. The faithful of any age, or of either sex, may belong to the association. When a person becomes a member, their name is entered on the register, and with their certificate of admission, they are also given a copy of the Statutes and rules.

V. The principal Feast of the Archconfraternity is that of Saint Peter, in whose Church at Rome the veil of Saint Veronica is preserved, while its lesser feasts are those of the Crown of Thorns and the Transfiguration. Moreover, special homage is paid to the Holy Face on Good Friday when the Church commemorates the insults our Blessed Lord endured for us and specially the Outrages offered to His Sacred Face, and also on Easter Sunday when the veil of St. Veronica is publicly exhibited at Rome in presence of the Sovereign Pontiff.

VI.   The members meet once a month, the day and time, together with the prayers and ceremonies being fixed by the director, with the approbation of the Ordinary.

VII.   The director is appointed by the Ordinary, and either he, or his deputy, has the power to enroll members and to sign their certificates of admission.

Examined and approved:

On the vigil of the Feast of the Patronage of the Blessed Virgin.

Tours, October 26th, 1885

✝ GUILLAUME-RENE
Archbishop of Tours

INDULGENCES GRANTED
BY POPE LEO XIII

Manual of the Archconfraternity of the Holy Face 1887, pgs. 55-56

(Applicable to the souls in purgatory)

Plenary Indulgences:
1. On the day of admission (In order that the associate may more easily gain this plenary indulgence, unless advised to the contrary, the Director will name, for the day of his admission, a Sunday or Festival).
2. At the hour of death.
3. For every yearly pilgrimage made to the Oratory of the Holy Face.
4. On the feast of St. Peter, or on a day during the Octave.
5. On the feast of the Transfiguration, or a day during the Octave.
6. On Passion Sunday, or any other day fixed by the Ordinary.

In order to gain these last three indulgences, it is necessary to visit the seat of the Confraternity.

Partial Indulgences:

Seven years and seven quarantines: for each assistance at the monthly reunions.

Sixty days:
1. For each pious exercise performed at the seat of the Confraternity.
2. For any other work of piety offered in union with the object of the association.
3. Each time a member devoutly kisses the effigy of the Holy Face repeating the invocation: *Lord, show us They Face, and we shall be saved.*

Hundred days: for every prayer said before an effigy of the Holy Face. (*Pius IX. December 11, 1876.*)

Forty days: each time a member assists at any of the daily morning or evening exercises in the chapel of the Holy Face at Tours. (*The Archbishop of Tours, November 15, 1876.*)

The above indulgences which require that a visit should be made to the church, may be gained by sick persons by virtue of some other act prescribed by the confessor. (*Brief of the 30th of March 1885.*)

N. B. The associates will endeavor to be faithful to their pious engagements, although these engagements, as they all know, do not impose an obligation of conscience, that is to say, do not oblige under penalty of sin.

Manual of the Archconfraternity of the Holy Face 1887, pgs. 65-85

I. Object of the Worship

The Archconfraternity of the Holy Face professes specially to worship the Holy Face of our Lord, outraged and disfigured in His Passion. Religion has no object more touching and more worthy of our homage.

In the Old Testament mention is often made of the Face of God. In heaven, Angels and Cherubim adore It; upon earth, under whatever visible form it may appear, patriarchs, prophets and the just of all ages contemplate It with profound veneration and religious awe. But when the Son of God is incarnated, when the Word assumes the figure and the resemblance of man, the Divine Face, in the person of Jesus, becomes an object of admiration, of respect and of love; first to Mary and Joseph, then to the disciples and to all who behold It and who appreciate Its ravishing features and Its ineffable beauty. At Bethlehem, at Nazareth, on Tabor, in the different states through which It passed, this august Face, the mirror of the holiest of souls and of the most tender of hearts, merits to be contemplated and adored.

It above all deserves to be so in the humiliating and sorrowful state to which It was subjected during the Passion. Our Lord, in no other portion of His Holy Humanity, suffered so much as He did in His amiable Face. From the Garden of Olives, where the adorable Face was covered with a sweat of blood and defiled by the traitorous kiss of Judas, to the last sigh which It exhaled at the moment of death, when It was bowed down upon the Cross, there was no species of abasement, ignominy and suffering to which Jesus did not voluntarily submit It. His head and His forehead were crowned with thorns, His eyes bathed with bitter tears, His lips steeped in gall and vinegar; blows, spittle, the most savage outrages were inflicted upon Him. "We have seen Him," says the prophet, "and there was no beauty in Him that we should desire Him. He was despised and rejected of men." The evangelists expressly say that the impious spit in His Face and buffeted Him and struck His Face with the palms of their hands, saying: "Prophesy unto us, O Christ, who is he that struck Thee?" and, again spitting upon Him, they took the reed and struck His head. These minute details, at once so expressive and affecting, were not written and consigned to the Holy Scriptures without a particular design of God. They eloquently exhort us to give, whilst meditating on the different mysteries of the Passion of the Savior, a special attention to the aspect and the worship of His sorrowful Face.

II. Practical Object

The homage which we render to the suffering Face of the Redeemer has an eminently practical object and a very real one. It is that of offering to the Divine Majesty, which has been offended, a just reparation for the inexpressible outrages which the impiety of the present time is not afraid, whether in secret or in public, of inflicting upon the sovereignty of God, on the Divinity of Jesus Christ, on all that is religious and sacred. Amongst the special crimes belonging to the time in which we live, we must include blasphemy and the profanation of Sunday.

In our days blasphemy is committed with unheard of audacity. Not content with outraging the most adorable and thrice Holy Name of God, the modern blasphemer attacks God personally; he combats Christ in the truth of doctrine, in the morals of His Gospel, in the practice of His Sacraments, in the rights and even in the very existence of His Church. Not to speak of gross blasphemy, properly so called, which we so often hear resounding in our ears, and which seems to be vomited from out the mouth of hell, but blasphemy which assumes to be doctrinal and scientific, is uttered privately in the secret societies or pompously in public discourses; it is printed and displays itself in the light of day, in newspapers, pamphlets and books; it poisons and perverts all conditions and all ages.

The violation of Sunday does not show a less undisguised contempt for the law of God and His sovereign authority. The sanctification and repose of the seventh day are no longer observed except by a small number of Christians worthy of the name. Holy Days are profaned with a kind of indifference, deliberately and without remorse, in the workshop of the artisan and the counting house of the merchant, in the interior of families and in public places, in populous cities and in the smallest hamlets.

The infraction of these Divine commandments has risen to a state of social crime. It took place formerly, it is true, but never was it committed in so general a manner as at the present day. Evidently, such a state of things, so contrary to the fundamental economy of religion, overthrows at once the moral order of society, ruins the family to its foundations, and provokes the vengeance of Heaven. Such crimes cannot remain unpunished here below; they must be expiated, either by the scourge of Divine Justice or by voluntary reparation.

This reparation is an absolute and urgent necessity. At the present moment, there is not a single Catholic who does not loudly proclaim it to be so. The prosperity and peace of nations are obtainable only at this price.

What then must we do? The example given us by our enemies may serve as a lesson to us. We see them taking counsel with each other and concerting together, in freemasonry and the secret societies, men, blaspheming and profaning all that is most sacred, give each other the password, and link themselves together by an infernal compact; they have already reached the point of no longer dissimulating their projects; they form in the face of day frightful plots against the Lord and His Christ. Is not this then the moment for the children of God, for whoever has at heart the salvation of his brethren and the regeneration of society, to unite in the Name, and under the auspices of the august Face, so shamefully outraged, in order to erect a rampart against the torrents of Divine anger which ceaselessly accumulate against us and threaten to overwhelm us? Was ever a society of reparation more necessary? Could Providence offer us a more opportune aid, and one in closer connection with our pressing needs?

III. The Means of Reparation

The means of making effectual reparation for the crimes of which we have just spoken is to be found in a manner equally touching and admirable in the worship of the Holy Face, as understood and practiced in our Archconfraternity.

At all times there have been in the Church chosen souls, like Saint Augustine and Saint Gertrude, who have been animated by a special veneration for the Divine Face of the Redeemer. There have even existed, at certain epochs, Confraternities having for their object Its glorification and the rendering of public homage to It. But to attach to so consoling a devotion an idea of reparation, of establishing a direct relation between the species of crime which most outrages the sovereign Majesty of God and the kind of insult which has the most ignominiously disfigured the Face of Jesus Christ, is a conception which belongs to our own times, and which characterizes our new Archconfraternity! It was necessary that blasphemy and the profanation of holy things should rise to a degree of scandal and of perversity unknown until now in order to enable Christian piety to look at the Face of Jesus under a fresh aspect, and thereby to open up a new means of reparation. Hitherto the salutary means contained in the devotion to the Holy Face had not been observed and turned to account. Perhaps It would not have been remarked, even now, had it not been for a special illumination communicated to a fervent Religious of the Carmel at Tours, Sister Marie de Saint-Pierre, and without the zeal of a great servant of God and St. Martin, Mr. Dupont, who during twenty-five years of his life, practiced acts of reparation before the Face of Jesus Christ. It was given to these two holy souls, vividly to see and feel all the power and reality existing in this means of reparation; they practiced it themselves and transmitted it to others.

It was felt that fresh needs require new remedies. Therefore, the devotion to the Holy Face enters naturally, as it were, into the souls of men and is everywhere received with eagerness and confidence. Accepting its reparatory character, the Archconfraternity of the Holy Face presents to the Heavenly Father the adorable Face of our Lord, such as It was in the days of Its Passion, wounded, spit upon, covered with sweat and with blood. "O Father, It exclaims, look on the Face of Thy only and well-beloved Son; of Him who is the 'image of Thy greatness,' and the splendor of Thy glory. He has suffered for us, He has expiated our ingratitude and our crimes, look on Him and forgive us. *Respice in Faciem Christi tui.* And Thou, merciful Face of Jesus, show us what Thou art, and we shall be saved. *Ostende Faciem tuam, et salvi erimus.*"

These beautiful invocations which the Church utters so often in her Psalms, have become the watchword and the motto of our Archconfraternity. They express all that this means of reparation, placed at our disposition, contains of consolation and of hope. The scars imprinted on the disfigured Face of the Redeemer, the tears, the sweat and the blood which flow from His loving and compassionate Face, offer to the associates a rich treasure, an inexhaustible mine of merits and of satisfactions, wherewith to pay their debt to Divine Justice. Let us then approach It with confidence, let us render It our homage; let us make use of this powerful advocate in order to plead our cause; the Father will "look on the Face of His Christ, and we shall be saved."

IV. Models of Reparation

Our Lord has Himself willed to point out to us, what is, in regard to Him, the best means of reparation, first by raising up upon the road to Calvary a pious woman who offered Him the solace of which He stood in need. Veronica perceives Him laden with His Cross, climbing the mountain of His sacrifice; His Face soiled, wounded, bleeding. Listening only to her compassion and her piety, the courageous Israelite braves the raillery of her fellow citizens, and the brutality of the executioners, and, making her way through the crowd, draws nigh to Him; she detaches the veil of fine Egyptian linen which covers her head, spreads it over the wounded Face of the Savior, gently wipes with it His adorable Face, solacing, comforting and reanimating it. This was the first homage of reparation offered to our well-beloved Redeemer on the path of sorrows; He showed His gratitude for it, and as a recompense He left on the veil of His compassionate benefactress the impression of His Holy Face in the state to which It had been reduced.

Tradition has transmitted to us this memorable fact; it is, in the exercises of the Way of the Cross, the subject of the sixth station, and the precious veil, with the miraculous image imprinted upon it, is kept, at the present day, in the Church of St Peter at Rome, where, from time immemorial, it has been an object of supreme honor. Veronica herself, according to the communications made to Sister Marie de Saint-Pierre, is given us by our Lord as the model of the reparatory souls of which our epoch stands in need upon that other Calvary which the Church is climbing in the 19th century; and her example should encourage Christians who feel themselves to be inspired with the desire to compensate the Savior for the outrages committed against His majesty. The recompense bestowed upon her is the exterior symbol of the spiritual graces which we are sure to obtain by devoting ourselves to the work of reparation.

Another model is given us in the person of the Good Thief, who from the cross as from a pulpit, spoke in defense of the cause of Christ, and confessed His Divinity at the very moment when it was blasphemed by the other thief and by the multitude of the impious. Turning a reverential and a suppliant countenance towards the sorrowful and wounded Face of Jesus: "Lord," he said, "remember me when Thou shalt come into Thy kingdom." His prayer is granted at that very moment. The Face of the Lord inclines Itself towards him and His lips utter those ineffable words which ensure to this model of reparatory souls, as a supreme recompense, the immediate vision of His glorious Face: *Amen, I say to thee, this day thou shall be with Me in Paradise.*

The fathers of the Church are inexhaustible in their praise of the Good Thief. Saint John Chrysostom, when meditating upon his faith, raises it above that of Abraham, of Moses and of Isaiah. "They," he says, "saw Christ upon the throne and in the bosom of His glory and they believed he sees Him in the midst of torments, and he adores Him as though He were in glory; he sees Him on His cross, and he prays to Him as though He were seated in the highest heavens; he sees a criminal, and he invokes a King…" According to the same father, the Good Thief became at once an "evangelist" and a "prophet"; he preaches the Divine Crucified, he announces His eternal Kingdom.

Tradition knows him under the name of Dysmas. The Roman martyrology inscribes him amongst the saints of the 25th of March, and the Breviary, in the "Proper particular to some places," assigns him an office and indicates his feast as that of a double on the 24th of April. This prayer contains a significant expression; the Church asks: "God, who justifies sinners, to provoke us to repentance by means *of the compassionate aspect of His only Son which attracted the blessed thief*, and to grant us the same eternal glory." It would be impossible to offer to the Catholics of our days, to the zealots and apostles of the Reparation, a more worthy and better authorized model.

V. Picture Adopted by the Archconfraternity

The picture adopted as a type by the Archconfraternity is the representation of the august Face of the Savior, as it was visibly impressed upon the veil of Saint Veronica. This picture is venerated at Rome, in equal degree with the wood of the true Cross and the iron of the holy spear; it ranks amongst the great relics which are exhibited on certain days with great solemnity in the Vatican Basilica. *The copies which are painted on linen or silk, if they are furnished with a seal of authentication, enjoy the same privileges as the miraculous picture itself, and, according to the rules of the liturgy, ought to be equally honored; therefore, it is not proper to expose them to public veneration unless a lamp or a taper be kept constantly burning before them.*

Since the exile of Pius IX at Gaeta, in 1848, in consequence of circumstances connected with the misfortunes of those days, these venerable copies of the Vatican picture have been diffused in great numbers amongst the faithful and above all in France.

One of the first sent from Rome providentially fell into the hands of Mr. Dupont in the year 1851. That great servant of God and fervent apostle of the reparation placed It in a position where It could be plainly seen in his drawing room; then he lighted a lamp before It, which he kept burning day and night, and during twenty-five years he never ceased to honor It and obtain by Its means graces and favors of all kinds

Christian art, it is well known, takes pleasure in representing the Divine Face of the Savior under several different aspects; sometimes it is the Face of the *Ecce Homo*, otherwise called the "Christ of the Reed" wearing on his brow the crown of thorns, and sometimes the veil with which the soldiers blindfolded Him; sometimes it is the Face of the *Orante*, or the Savior in the attitude of prayer, as it is seen in the catacombs; at other times, it is the head of Christ on the Cross, or yet again, the Face of the Man God radiant with glory and majesty as on Tabor, or lastly the Face of the Infant Jesus in His cradle, or in the arms of His mother. Expressive and touching as are these different representations, the Archconfraternity, in view of the object which it proposes to itself, prefers to them the *facsimile* of the veil of Veronica.

87

If, in fact, we look at this holy picture with the eyes of faith, we shall, recognize, even from the point of view of art and without speaking of its antiquity and its miraculous origin, that it is very touching in its aspect, and well calculated to induce souls to perform acts of reparation; it is impossible to consider, without a profound feeling of compunction, the bleeding forehead of the Savior, the swollen and half closed eyes, the livid and darkened countenance. On the right cheek, in addition to the wounds, may be clearly distinguished the impress of the gauntlet of iron worn on the hand which struck Him so cruelly in the house of Annas, and on the other cheek traces of spittle. The nose is wounded and bleeding, the mouth open and filled with blood; the teeth are broken, the head and the hair torn out in different places Thus changed and disfigured, the most Holy Face of Jesus does none the less present to us, in Its whole aspect, an ineffable mixture of greatness, of compassion, of love and of sorrow, which touches the hearts of all who look upon It. Beneath those bleeding wounds and that ignoble spittle, the Christian soul recognizes the majesty of its God, and, touched with repentance at the sight of so striking an expiation of its ingratitude, it abandons itself without reserve, to a sweet confidence and an ardent love for its Redeemer.

VI. Cross of the Archconfraternity

The Archconfraternity, having its center in the archiepiscopal city of Tours where it had its origin, adopts as a principal sign of decoration for its members a cross with two arms arranged in the manner shown; on the center of one of its sides is inscribed the monogram of Christ surrounded with the words: *Reparation Pie IX* 1847, and upon the arms of the cross: *Sit nomen Domini benedictum*; on the obverse is seen engraved, on the center, the Holy Face, above which is the inscription of the Cross: *INRI*, and beneath: *Vade retro, Satana*. The associates are advised habitually to wear this cross as a safeguard; during pilgrimages and at public ceremonies, it is well to have it placed where it can be seen on the breast. The Archconfraternity is an army; the cross, such as it has been described, is its standard; let us wear it with confidence; it will help us to conquer our enemies and to repair our losses. But it is not absolutely necessary that the cross should be worn; according to the rule, it may be replaced by a medal or a scapular of the Holy Face.

VII. Advantages of the Archconfraternity

To honor the august Face of the Redeemer by performing at the present day the same office in regard to It which the pious Veronica fulfilled on Calvary, to render ourselves useful to the Church, to society and to souls, by endeavoring to repair the crimes which do the greatest amount of evil to our contemporaries; these two acts, so noble and meritorious in themselves, become a source of graces and benedictions for fervent souls who devote themselves to the work. To these advantages may be added the numerous indulgences whether partial or plenary which the Church grants to the associates; and the participation in the ineffable promises made by our Lord to all those who honor His most Holy Face.

VIII. Engravings of the Holy Face

The engravings of the Holy Face are the reproduction of the veil of Veronica at the Vatican. No one is ignorant of the respect paid by the Church to the relic. Every year, two Cardinals,   delegated for that purpose, give the same benediction with it to the kneeling people, as that given with the Blessed Sacrament, and with the sacred wood of the true Cross. An authentic attes-

VERA EFFIGIES SACRI VULTUS DOMINI NOSTRI JESU CHRISTI

tation of the Divinity of Jesus Christ, this blessed veil has been left to the Church, to be, as it were, a precious coin, marked with the effigy of the King of kings, intended to call down upon the world, which is ceaselessly impending towards its ruin, the mercies of the Lord.

Earthly coins have engraved upon them the effigy of their princes, in order to enable the kingdoms of the world freely to exchange their different products. Wherefore then, should not the kingdom of heaven also have, like the kingdoms of the earth, a coin by means of which everlasting goods may be purchased? *O God! Our Protector, look upon us, and cast Thine eyes upon the Face of Thy Christ*, ought to be our frequent cry.

Every soul attached to Holy Church, and with it to the dogma of the Divinity of our Lord, ought to make it a law of love, to have in its own little oratory a picture of the *Holy Face*. Ah! If this devotion did but reign in all hearts, we should soon see the last remnants disappear of the odious blasphemy which has come down even to our own days: the denial namely of the Divinity of Jesus! The devotion to the Holy Face is a sign of predestination, for what soul is there which after having loved and venerated this *august Face* on earth may not rest assured of one day venerating It amidst the triumphs of Its glory? (*Letter of Mr. Dupont.*)

N.B. These engravings come from Rome, where they are engraved under the guarantee of the proper authority. Moreover, they have attached to them an authentication bearing the signature and the seal of a Cardinal, attesting that they have touched the veil of Veronica, the wood of the true Cross and the iron of the spear which transfixed our Lord. This authentication ought to be carefully preserved. The word *gratis*, painted on them in large characters, is to show that the favor of touching these holy relics is gratuitously bestowed, and that the blessing attached thereto is not sold; but it does not mean to imply that the engravings themselves are not to be sold at a proper price, calculated to cover the expenses of the paper, linen or silk of the engraving, of the carriage, etc.; these prices are, moreover, made as low as possible and ought never to be an object of speculation.[115]

[115] The Manual of the Holy Face, A.M.P., p. 92-93

PROMISES OF OUR LORD JESUS CHRIST IN FAVOR OF ALL WHO HONOR HIS HOLY FACE

Manual of the Archconfraternity of the Holy Face 1887, pgs. 86-88

1. They shall receive in themselves, by the impression of My Humanity, a bright irradiation from My Divinity, and shall be so illuminated by it in their inmost souls that by their likeness to My Face they shall shine with a brightness surpassing that of many others in eternal life. (St. Gertrude, *Insinuations,* book IV, ch. VII)

2. St. Mechtilde having asked our Lord that those who celebrate the memory of His sweet Face should never be deprived of His amiable company, He replied: "Not one of them shall be separated from Me." (St. Mechtilde, *De la Grace Spirituelle (Of Spiritual Grace),* book I, ch. XIII)

3. "Our Lord," said Sister Marie de Saint-Pierre, "has promised me that He will imprint His Divine likeness on the souls of those who honor His most Holy Countenance." (January 21, 1847) "This adorable Face is, as it were, the seal of the Divinity, which has the virtue of reproducing the likeness of God in the souls that are applied to It." (November 6, 1845)

4. "By My Holy Face you shall work miracles." (Our Lord to Sister Marie de Saint-Pierre, October 27, 1845.)

5. "By My Holy Face you will obtain the conversion of many sinners. Nothing that you ask in making this offering will be refused to you. No one can know how pleasing the sight of My Face is to My Father!" (Our Lord to Sister Marie de Saint-Pierre, November 22, 1846)

6. "As in a kingdom you can procure all you wish for with a coin marked with the prince's effigy, so in the Kingdom of Heaven you will obtain all you desire with the precious coin of my Holy Humanity, which is My adorable Countenance." (Our Lord to Sister Marie de Saint-Pierre, October 29, 1845)

7. "All those who honor My Holy Face in a spirit of reparation will by so doing perform the office of the pious Veronica." (Our Lord to Sister Marie de Saint-Pierre, October 27, 1845)

8. "According to the care you take in making reparation to My Face, disfigured by blasphemies, so will I take care of your soul, which has been disfigured by sin. I will reprint My image and render it as beautiful as it was on leaving the baptismal font." (Our Lord to Sister Marie de Saint-Pierre, November 3, 1845)

9. "Our Lord has promised me," said again Sister Saint-Pierre, "for all those who defend His cause in this Work of Reparation, by words, by prayers, or in writing, that He will defend them before His Father; at their death He will purify their souls by effacing all the blots of sin and will restore to them their primitive beauty." (March 12, 1846)

SAINT THERESE OF THE CHILD JESUS
AND OF THE HOLY FACE
1888 - Enters Carmel

1873 - 1897

St. Therese of Lisieux was born on January 2, 1873. She was the last of nine children born to the Martin family.

Little Therese, at the age of only four years old, lost her mother. Even at this young age she formed a strong devotion to our blessed Mother Mary, relying on her for help during this devastating loss.

By the time Therese was twelve years old, she was accustomed to venerating the Holy Face of Jesus with her family, as it was represented on the veil of Veronica. On April 26, 1885, Therese, her sisters Marie, Leonie, and Celine, as well as her father, were enrolled in the Confraternity of the Holy Face in Tours. In that same year, Pope Leo XIII raised it to the status of Archconfraternity and established it for the entire world.

At the age of fourteen, Therese expressed to her father her desire to enter Carmel. She would be the fourth daughter of the family to enter a religious order. Since the Carmelite Rule stipulated sixteen as the accepted age for entrance, Therese and her father had to overcome tremendous obstacles to make this a reality.

Over several months, her request to enter Carmel was rejected by both their priest and then their bishop. Therese and her father took the last recourse open to them and decided to ask permission from the Holy Father, Pope Leo XIII.

Therese and her sister Celine, left with their father on their journey, joining the pilgrimage especially organized to commemorate the Pope's Golden Jubilee.[116]

The Martins and other pilgrims assembled for the great audience with Pope Leo...one after another they came before the Holy Father.[117]

After Louis Martin and Celine, Therese knelt at the foot of the Papal throne. Turning imploring eyes to the Supreme Pontiff, Therese said: "Holy Father, I have a great favor to ask of you... I beg you to allow me to enter Carmel at the age of fifteen... If only you were to say 'Yes,' everyone else would be willing...."

"Child, you will enter if it be God's will..." the Pope replied with sympathy... The Holy Father then placed his hand on Therese's lips, then raised it in blessing over her head.[118]

---

[116] The Whole World Will Love Me, The Life of St. Therese of the Child Jesus and of the Holy Face, Dorothy Scallan, Tan Books and Publishers, Inc., p. 153

[117] The Whole World Will Love Me, p. 154

[118] The Whole World Will Love Me, p. 155-156

Finally, on January 1st, the day before Therese's fifteenth birthday, she received the answer to her prayers. It was a letter from the prioress of the Carmelite Convent, Mother Mary Gonzaga, notifying her that she had permission from the bishop to enter.

Three months later, on April 9, 1888, Therese entered the Lisieux convent as a novice. She recalls... "No more waiting now for the fulfilment of my ambitions; I can't tell you what a deep and refreshing sense of peace this thought carried with it. And, deep down, this sense of peace has been a lasting possession; it's never left me, even when my trials have been most severe."[119]

Sister Therese on wash day (second from left)

A few months after St. Therese entered the convent, Sr. Agnes (Therese's sister Pauline) asked the prioress for

[119] Autobiography of St. Therese of Lisieux, translated by Ronald Knox, P.J. Kenedy & Sons, 1958, p. 183-184

permission to give Therese the book which had recently been published "Life of Sr. Marie Pierre", and to be allowed to instruct her in the Holy Face Devotion

To trace its history, at Lisieux, the Holy Face devotion had already taken deep roots. The foundress of the Carmel of Lisieux, Mother Genevieve, as early as 1847 (while Sister Marie Pierre still lived in her Tours cloister), had already accepted the Revelations concerning Reparation through devotion to the Holy Face... Without delay, she got the picture of the Holy Face, and had exposed it in the public chapel of the convent... Mother Genevieve had at once embraced it for herself and her convent both privately and publicly.[120]

Now, many years later (around 1876), although Mother Genevieve was old and confined in the infirmary, she had hopes for a young novice, Sister Agnes (St. Therese's sister) who showed rare spiritual discernment. Mother Genevieve now encouraged her to pin her gaze on the Face of Jesus and keep it there in a spirit of Reparation. Young Sister Agnes obeyed, and discovered a world of new meaning in her vocation. When her youngest sister, Therese, entered Carmel a few short years later, she enjoined her to embrace it as well.[121]

St. Therese's words: "Until then I had not appreciated the beauties of the Holy Face, and it was you my little Mother (Sr. Agnes), who unveiled them to me. Just as you

---

[120] The Whole World Will Love Me, p. 211

[121] The Whole World Will Love Me, p. 215

had been the first to leave our home for Carmel, so, too, were you the first to penetrate the mysteries of love hidden in the Face of our Divine Spouse..."[122]

The day of Sister Therese's investiture was January 10, 1889. This was the Clothing Ceremony, the end of which was to transform a person of the world into a religious of Mount Carmel. (It was expected that Sister Therese would have the name Sr. Therese of the Child Jesus, but at her investiture she chose to add the object of her adoration to her name.) On that day Sister Therese became Sister Therese of the Child Jesus and of the Holy Face.[123]

It took an additional eight months before Sister Therese was permitted to take her Profession of Vows. Before doing so, she was required to go through a ten-day retreat to withdraw within herself with no distractions. She used this time to meditate on our Lord's Holy Face as the Supreme Object of her Adoration. The evening before her Profession a darkness consumed her, and she felt she couldn't take her vows. She held the small Holy Face that she kept and prayed for help. Immediately the darkness left her soul.

In January of 1895, in obedience to Mother Agnes, Sister Therese began writing her manuscripts. This was done in three parts: 1. Manuscript A – memoirs of her childhood, 2. Manuscript B – which Therese entitled "My Vocation: Love" (which she began in 1896 after her first

---

[122] The Whole World Will Love Me, p. 216

[123] The Whole World Will Love Me, p. 197

symptoms of tuberculosis), and 3. Manuscript C - (which she began writing in June of 1897, less than three months before her death.)

Consecration to the Holy Face
Handwritten by St. Therese August 6, 1896.
Therese (far right), her sister Celine (Sr. Genevieve).
and her sister Louise (Sr. Marie).

St. Therese's "Little Way"

Saint Therese lived her religious life as a "little flower" of Christ, often referring to herself as such. She considered herself so small and insignificant, that she was like a little flower that needed nurturing and water to grow. The following is from her Manuscript addressed to Mother Marie de Gonzaga, who was her prioress at the time (June 1897):

...I think about the firm motherly discipline I had from you... Jesus knew well enough that the little flower he had planted was in need of watering; only the waters of humiliation could revive it--it was too weak a plant to take root without being helped in this way. And it was through you, Mother, that this blessing was bestowed.[124]

As you know, dear Mother, I've always wished that I could be a saint. But whenever I compared myself to the Saints there was always this unfortunate difference – they were like great mountains, hiding their heads in the clouds, and I was only an insignificant grain of sand, trodden down by all who passed by.... Obviously, there's nothing great to be made of me, so it must be possible for me to aspire to sanctity in spite of my insignificance. I've got to take myself just as I am, with all my imperfections... Can't I find a lift which will take me up to Jesus since I'm not big enough to climb the steep stairway of perfection?... Eternal Wisdom says: "Is anyone simple as a little child? Then let him come to me."...I could after all be lifted up to heaven in the arms of Jesus! And if that was to happen, there was no need for me to grow bigger; on the contrary, I must be as small as ever, smaller than ever.[125]

Sister Therese lived her life committed to her "little way" through constant little acts of love and charity. Any and every task, no matter how big or how small, was enthusiastically done for Jesus with great love. She taught her "little way" to all of her fellow Sisters in Carmel with humility, generosity, and love.

---

[124] Autobiography of St. Therese of Lisieux, Kenedy & Sons, p. 246

[125] Autobiography of St. Therese of Lisieux, Kenedy & Sons, p. 248-249

*"Our Lord does not look so much
at the greatness of our actions, nor even the difficulty,
but at the love with which we do them."*

– St. Therese of Lisieux

ST. THERESE'S ILLNESS AND DEATH
SHE DIED IN THE ODOR OF SANCTITY SEPTEMBER 30, 1897

In April of 1896, Saint Therese had her first symptom of tuberculosis. A hemoptysis episode, where the person coughs up blood from a hemorrhage in the lungs. She informed the newly elected Mother Superior, Mother Mary Gonzaga, of the episode. In obedience to her Prioress, Sister Therese kept the secret of her condition  hidden from her Sisters in the convent, as well as from her own sisters, Mother Agnes (Pauline), Sister Marie (Louise), and Sister Genevieve (Celine).

Another month passed. Sr. Therese was now coughing noticeably. The Convent's physician was consulted, but neither the physician nor her family were told of the hemorrhages. The next fall and winter she continued to fail in her strength.[126] However, since she was still doing her work and taking walks in the garden, everyone had hope that she would recover. It was not until May before her health deteriorated to the point where her illness could no longer be concealed, that Mother Agnes and her two other sisters were told of her true condition.

As Sister Therese's suffering grew worse, she said these words to Mother Agnes, "*After my death I will let fall a shower of roses....*" On July 17, 1897, she said: "*I feel that my mission is soon to begin. to make others love God as I do, to teach others my 'Little Way'. I will spend my Heaven in doing good upon earth...*"[127]

Saint Therese suffered terrible darkness for a year and a half before her death, allowing no one to know of it. The enemy besieged her with doubts about God's very existence and of an afterlife. Since she was still writing her manuscripts during this time, she wrote of this blackness. "*Our Lord allowed my soul to be overrun by an impenetrable darkness, which made the thought of Heaven, hitherto so welcome. a subject of nothing but conflict and torment.*"[128]

...The mists around me have become denser than ever; they sink deep into my soul and wrap it round so that I can't even recover the dear image of my native country anymore — everything has disappeared... It is worse torment than ever; the

---

[126] The Whole World Will Love Me, p.294

[127] The Autobiography of Therese of Lisieux, the Story of a Soul, translated by Michael Day, Dover Publications, p. 203

[128] Autobiography of St. Therese of Lisieux, Kenedy & Sons, p. 254

darkness itself seems to borrow from the sinners who live in it, the gift of speech..."[129]

The darkness culminated on the Feast of the Transfiguration, the special feast of all adorers of the Holy Face. Mother Agnes obtained permission to place a large picture of the true Image of Our Lord's Face, adorned with flowers, in her sister's sickroom...

"Never have I suffered more from temptations against faith than on this night of the Feast. But I never stopped looking at the Holy Face and making acts of faith!"[130]

During her entire hidden life at Carmel, Sister Therese had consistently applied herself to penetrating the secrets contained in the Face of Christ, pondering His unspeakable mental anguish. Imitating her model, who gave the world the incomparable revelations on the efficacy of Devotion to the Holy Face of Christ....[131]

On the evening of September 30, 1897, Therese's suffering came to an end. Her last words were, "Oh, I love Him!... My God... I love You!"[132]

---

[129] Autobiography of St. Therese of Lisieux, Kenedy & Sons, p. 255

[130] The Whole World Will Love Me, p. 305

[131] The Whole World Will Love Me, p. 312

[132] Archives Du Carmel De Lisieux, archives-carmel-lisieux.fr, Last Words With Celine (Sr. Genevieve), 1897

7 THE SHROUD OF TURIN
1898 – the Shroud was Photographed for the First Time

As children of God, we were truly blessed by our Lord Jesus Christ on the day of His Passion, when He gave us the gift of His Holy Face twice, once while still alive on the Veil of Veronica, and again after death on the Holy Shroud.

The following excerpts are from an article entitled:
"What is the Shroud of Turin? Facts & History Everyone Should Know"
by Myra Adams and Russ Breult, Nov. 8, 2019, Christianity.com.

The holy relic of the Shroud of Turin has resided in the Cathedral of St. John the Baptist in Turin, Italy, since 1578.

In 1898, an Italian named Secondo Pia photographed the Shroud for the first time. The cloth's faint yellowed image, as seen with the naked eye, is actually a *negative image* that, when developed, turns into a detailed black and white *positive.* Pia's unexplainable discovery startled him, along with Church authorities and the scientific community.

Can it be proved that the image of "the Man of the Shroud" is Jesus Christ? Only by inference according to the four gospels (along with the details on the Shroud):

- Bloodstains on the head compatible with a crown of thorns.
- Over 120 scourge marks compatible with Roman flagrum.
- Nail wound in the wrists (more anatomically correct to hold the weight of the body than the palm of the hand).
- Nail wound in the feet. (The feet were on top of each other.)
- Legs are pulled up due to rigor mortis. (A stiffness of muscles that sets in quickly after death and lasts less than four days.)
- Blood is sourced from actual wounds showing evidence of gravity from a vertical position.
- No stains of body decomposition. (Resurrection happened on the third day before decomposition had time to occur.)
- Wound in the side compatible in size with a Roman spear tip.
- Post-mortem blood flow from the side wound that also flows across the back.
- Legs were not broken. (Old Testament prophecy fulfilled.)

Except for Jesus, there is no man in recorded Roman history who was severely scourged and crucified. Normally, it was one punishment or the other. The Man of the Shroud endured both as written in the gospels.

The Shroud still exists, and we would argue for *divine reason*. And by its very existence, proves that the cloth has been "protected" after being hidden in a wall in Edessa for over 400 years and then surviving through crusades, wars, numerous fires, and even Hitler.

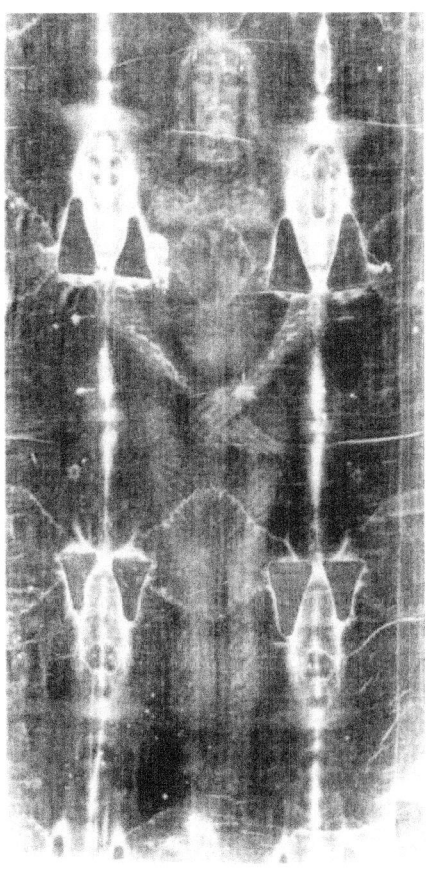

It is important to note that there were medals of the Holy Face cast in the time of Pope Innocent III (1198-1216 A.D.), which were called Veronicas (see page 16). Holy Face medals were also made in the mid to late 1800s using the image from the Veil of Veronca which the Archconfraternity of the Holy Face approved as one of the objects of Reparation. However, after several years passed, the medals were no longer made. It wasn't until 1936, when Sr. Maria Pierina received her revelations, that she revived the medal and chose the image on the Shroud. The images from the Veil and the Shroud, are both the true Holy Face of Jesus, and both should be shown proper veneration.

1890 - 1945

Sister Maria Pierina was born in Milan, Italy in 1890. She was baptized on the same day and given the name Gliuseppina De Micheli. At a young age, she was raised to know the Holy Face devotion which had been started almost a century before.

On Good Friday at the age of twelve, something extraordinary happened. In the church of San Pietro in Sala, during the evening Adoration of the Cross. Gliuseppina was among the faithful who were in line to kiss the Crucifix (placed on the ground to be easily kissed on the body's wounds) when she heard a voice say to her: *"Nobody gives me a kiss of love on the face to repair Judas' kiss?"* She was amazed that no one had heard the voice. To herself, she said: *"I will give you the kiss of love Jesus, have patience!"* This moment was decisive for her religious journey.

In October of 1913, she entered the convent (the Congregation of the Daughters of the Immaculate Conception). As a novice she was permitted to do night adoration. On the night between Holy Thursday and Good Friday, while she was praying before the Crucifix, she heard it say, *"Kiss Me."* Sister Maria Pierina obeyed, and her lips felt not the contact with the image of plaster but the contact of the true face of Jesus.

She made her vows in May of 1914 and took the name Sister Maria Pierina. She was then sent to the motherhouse in Buenos Aires, Argentina where she remained until 1921. While there, her attachment to the Holy Face devotion grew stronger. In 1928, she was elected as the new Superior with full consent of all the members of the Congregation and became Mother Maria Pierina.

In a vision she was urged by the Blessed Mother and Jesus Himself to spread the devotion to the Holy Face in reparation for the insults our Lord suffered in His Passion, as well as for the many sins being committed against God in modern times.[133]

On May 23, 1936, Jesus appeared to Mother Pierina with bloodstained face and said, *"To thee I renew the offering of My Face, in order that thou mayest offer it without*

---

[133] The Devotion to the Holy Face as Revealed to Blessed Maria Pierina, literature printed by the Holy Face Association, Champlain, NY, and Montreal, Quebec, Canada, www.holyface.com

ceasing to the Eternal Father; with this offering thou wilt obtain the salvation and sanctification of many souls; when, however thou wilt offer it through my Priests, miracles will be worked."

On May 31st, the Immaculate Virgin appeared to her. She had in her hand a scapular, formed of two pieces of white flannel joined by a cord. On one side was impressed the Image of the Holy Face, having these words around it, *"Illumina, Domine, vultum tuum super nos."* ("May, O Lord, the light of Thy countenance shine upon us."), and in the other a sacred host surrounded by rays of light, having this writing round it, *"Mane nobiscum, Domine."* ("Stay with us, O Lord."). Mary told Mother Pierina, "Whoever wears this scapular and, if possible, pays a weekly visit to the Blessed Sacrament on Tuesday in a spirit of reparation for the outrages received by the Holy Face of our Blessed Savior during His Passion and those bestowed on Him every day in The Sacrament of His divine love, will be granted the gift of a strong Faith and the grace to fly to its defense conquering if need be all interior and exterior difficulties. Moreover, they are promised a happy death with special assistance of Christ Himself." [134]

It would be two more years before Mother Pierina was able to carry out our Blessed Mother Mary's request, not in the form of a scapular, but as a medal. On August 9, 1940, she obtained approval from the Curia to have the medals struck.[135] Even the expenses for the casting were

---

[134] The Story of Sister Maria Pierina De Micheli, Missionary – Messenger of the Holy Face of Jesus, by Sister Maria Idlefonsa Rigamonti, 1958, p. 70

[135] The Story of Sister Maria Pierina De Micheli, p. 91

miraculously met when she found on her desk an envelope with the exact amount of the bill – 11,200 lire.

After they were cast, the evil spirit showed his chagrin and rage at the medals by hurling them down and scattering them all over the floor.

Why did Mother Pierina circulate the medal and not the Scapular? In obedience to her Rev. Father Confessor, she wrote in her diary: "Continuing my prayer and turning to the Madonna to settle a doubt about the scapular, which I often ponder over, Mary said to me, "My daughter, be calm because the scapular is replaced by the medal. The medal carries the same promises and favors. It remains only to circulate it ever more widely."[136]

In our Blessed Mother's own words, the medal is a weapon for defense, a shield for courage, a token of love and mercy and which her Divine Son wished to give the world in these troubled days of lust and hatred for God and for His Church. Devilish snares have been set to rob the hearts of men of their faith while evil spreads the world over. Genuine apostles are few. A divine remedy to all these evils will be the Adorable Face of her Son, Jesus.

The very first new medal of the Holy Face was offered to our glorious Pontiff, Pope Pius XII; then the whole world got reacquainted with this special object of favors

---

[136] The Story of Sister Maria Pierina De Micheli, p. 92

and devotion. It is to be found on land and sea. Never has it been heard that a prisoner of war wearing this badge of salvation has been executed.[137]

Holy Face Medal of
Sr. Maria Pierina

Holy Face Medal
from the mid to late 1800s

Blessed Maria Pierina de Micheli died on July 26, 1945. She was beatified on the Solemnity of the Most Holy Trinity, Sunday, May 30th, 2010, at the Basilica of Santa Maria Maggiore in Rome by His Excellency, Archbishop Angelo Amato.

---

[137] The Devotion to the Holy Face as Revealed to Blessed Maria Pierina", holyface.com

CHAPLET OF THE HOLY FACE
Composed by Sister Mary of Saint Peter *(see page 25)*

*Explanation from the Manual of the Archconfraternity
of the Holy Face 1887, pgs. 233-235*

The little chaplet of the Holy Face has for its object the honoring of the five senses of our Lord Jesus Christ, and of entreating God for the triumph of his Church. This chaplet is composed of a cross and thirty-nine beads, six of which are large, and thirty-three small, and of a medal of the Holy Face. It is well to recite it every day, in order to obtain from God by means of the Face of His well-beloved Son, the triumph of our mother the Catholic Church, and the downfall of her enemies.

The Cross recalls to us the mystery of our Redemption; we must sign ourselves with it and make the invocation: *Deus, in adjutorium meum intende; Domine, at adjuvandum me festina*; followed by the Gloria Patri.

The thirty-three small beads represent the thirty-three years of the mortal life of our Lord. The first thirty recall to mind the thirty years of his private life, and are divided into five sixes with the intention of honoring the five senses of the *touch, hearing, sight, smell,* and *taste* of Jesus, which have their seat principally in His Holy Face, and of rendering homage to all the sufferings which our Lord endured in His Face, through each one of these senses. Each of these sixes is preceded by a large single bead in honor of the sense which it is intended to honor and is followed by a *Gloria Patri.*

The three small beads [by the crucifix] recall to mind the public life of the Savior and have for their object the honoring of all the wounds of His Adorable Face:

On each large single bead, must be said: *My Jesus, mercy!* (100 days of indulgence.) And on each small bead must be said: *Arise, O Lord, and let Thy enemies be scattered, and let all that hate Thee, flee from before Thy Face.* Note: St. Athanasius relates that when the devil was asked what verse in the whole Scripture was feared most, he replied that it was the words of the sixty-seventh Psalm that say: "Let God arise, and let His enemies be scattered; and let them that hate Him flee before His Face." The devil said that these are the words that always compel the evil spirits to take flight. When praying the chaplet, these words aren't intended to abandon the sinner, but to make the evil that is inside them flee.

The *Gloria* is said seven times [throughout the chaplet], in order to honor the seven words of Jesus upon the Cross, and the seven dolours of the Immaculate Virgin. When terminating it, we must say over the medal: *God, our Protector, look on us, and cast Thy eyes on the Face of Thy Christ.*

PRAY THE CHAPLET
(From the Discalced Carmelite Nuns)

Optional prayer of meditation that may be said before beginning the chaplet: *Lord, I offer this chaplet for the reparation of sin, for strength against the evil that prowls about the world seeking the ruin of souls, and for...* (add special intention here). *Accept this chaplet in honor of your five senses and all that You suffered through them on the day of Thy Passion.*

1. Make the Sign of the Cross and pray: *O Lord, make haste to come to my (our) aid.* Followed by the *Glory Be...*

2. On the single bead (in honor of His sense of sight) pray: *My Jesus, Mercy!* Followed by the *Glory Be...*

3. On each of the 6 beads pray: *Arise O Lord, and let Thy enemies be scattered, and let them that hate Thee, flee before Thy Face.*

4. On the single bead (in honor of His sense of smell) pray: *My Jesus, Mercy!* Followed by the *Glory Be...*

115

5. On each of the 6 beads pray: *Arise O Lord, and let Thy enemies be scattered, and let them that hate Thee, flee before Thy Face.*

6. On the single bead (in honor of His sense of taste) pray: *My Jesus, Mercy!* Followed by the *Glory Be…*

7. On each of the 6 beads pray: *Arise O Lord, and let Thy enemies be scattered, and let them that hate Thee, flee before Thy Face.*

8. On the single bead (in honor of His sense of hearing) pray: *My Jesus, Mercy!* Followed by the *Glory Be…*

9. On each of the 6 beads pray: *Arise O Lord, and let Thy enemies be scattered, and let them that hate Thee, flee before Thy Face.*

10. On the single bead (in honor of His sense of touch) pray: *My Jesus, Mercy!* Followed by the *Glory Be…*

11. On each of the 6 beads pray: *Arise O Lord, and let Thy enemies be scattered, and let them that hate Thee, flee before Thy Face.*

12. On the single bead pray: *My Jesus, Mercy!* Followed by the *Glory Be…*

13. On each of the 3 beads pray: *Arise O Lord, and let Thy enemies be scattered, and let them that hate Thee, flee before Thy Face.*

14. On the Holy Face Centerpiece or medal pray: *O God, our protector, Look on us, and on the Face of Thy Christ! Amen.*

THE GOLDEN ARROW
Dictated by our Lord to Sr. Mary of St. Peter

May the most holy, most sacred, most adorable,
most incomprehensible, and unutterable Name of God,
be always praised, blessed, loved, adored, and glorified,
in Heaven, on earth, and in the hells,
by all the creatures of God,
and by the Sacred Heart of our Lord Jesus Christ,
in the most Holy Sacrament of the Altar. Amen

PRAYERS TO BE SAID DAILY
TO PRACTICE THE HOLY FACE DEVOTION
As our Lord revealed to Sr. Mary (see pgs. 27-28)

Dear Lord, through the Sorrowful and Immaculate
Heart of Mary, I (we) offer You these prayers in
reparation for the sins which offend God in these
modern times — the sins of blasphemy
and the profanation of Sunday
and Your Holy Days of Obligation:

Say one *Our Father*, one *Hail Mary*, and one *Glory Be*,
followed by the Act of Praise, called the *Golden Arrow*
(above). On Sunday and on feast days, add the *Litany of
the Holy Face* (page 120 of this book).

AN ASPIRATION TO THE ETERNAL FATHER
To be frequently recited during the day

Eternal Father, we offer you the Holy Face of Jesus,
covered with blood, sweat, dust, and spittle,
in reparation for the crimes of communists,
blasphemers, and for the profaners of the
Holy Name and of the Holy Day. Amen

ACT OF LOVE TO THE HOLY FACE
*(Manual of the Archconfraternity
of the Holy Face 1887, p. 162)*

Adorable Face of my Jesus, my only love,
my light and my life, grant that I may see no one
except Thee, that I may know no one except Thee,
that I may love Thee alone, that I may live with Thee,
of Thee, by Thee, and for Thee. Amen.

By a Rescript dated 27th of January 1853, His Holiness
Pope Pius IX, grants to all who recite, with a contrite
heart, the following three prayers in honor of the Holy
Face of Jesus Christ, an indulgence of a hundred days for
each time; applicable to the souls in Purgatory.
*(Manual of the Archconfraternity
of the Holy Face, 1887, p 154-155)*

Prayer I

I salute Thee, I adore Thee, and I love Thee
O Jesus my Savior, outraged anew by blasphemers,
and I offer Thee, through the heart of
Thy blessed Mother, the worship of all the
Angels and Saints, most humbly beseeching Thee,
by virtue of Thy Sacred Face, to repair and renew in me
and in all men, Thy image disfigured by sin. Amen.

Pater, Ave, Gloria
(Say one Our Father, one Hail Mary, one Glory Be)

Prayer II

I salute Thee, I adore Thee, and I love Thee
O Adorable Face of Jesus, my Beloved,
Noble seal of the Divinity;
with all the powers of my soul I apply myself to Thee,
and most humbly pray Thee to imprint in us
all the features of Thy Divine likeness. Amen.

Prayer III

O Adorable Face of my Jesus,
so mercifully bowed down upon the tree of the Cross,
on the day of Thy Passion for the salvation of men,
now again, incline in Thy pity towards us poor sinners;
cast upon us a look of compassion,
and receive us to the kiss of peace. Amen.
Sacred Heart of Jesus, have Mercy on us. Amen.
Sit nomen Domini benedictum! Amen.

LITANY OF THE HOLY FACE OF JESUS

Composed by Sr. Mary of St. Peter - short version

O Jesus, whose Adorable Face was adored
with profound respect by Mary and Joseph
when they saw Thee for the first time,
have mercy on us.

O Jesus, whose Adorable Face, ravished with joy the Angels,
the shepherds, and the magi in the stable of Bethlehem,
have mercy on us.

O Jesus, whose Adorable Face, wounded with a dart of love
the aged Simeon and the prophetess Anna in the Temple,
have mercy on us.

O Jesus, whose Adorable Face, filled with admiration the
Doctors of the law in the Temple at the age of twelve years,
have mercy on us.

O Adorable Face, which possesses beauty
always ancient and always new,
have mercy on us.

O Jesus, whose Adorable Face is the masterpiece of the Holy
Ghost, in which the Eternal Father is well pleased,
have mercy on us.

O Jesus, whose Adorable Face is the ineffable mirror
of the Divine Perfections,
have mercy on us.

O Jesus, whose Adorable Face sorrowed and wept
at the tomb of Lazarus,
Have mercy on us.

O Jesus, whose Adorable Face, was brilliant like the sun
and radiant with glory on Mount Tabor,
have mercy on us.

O Jesus, whose Adorable Face grew sad at the sight of
Jerusalem, when Thou didst weep over that ungrateful city,
have mercy on us.

O Jesus, whose Adorable Face was bowed down to the
ground in the Garden of Olives,
and covered with confusion for our sins,
have mercy on us.

O Jesus, whose Adorable Face
was covered with the sweat of blood,
have mercy on us.

O Jesus, whose Adorable Face was kissed by Judas,
have mercy on us.

O Jesus, whose Adorable Face was struck by a vile servant,
shamefully blindfolded, and profaned
by the sacrilegious hands of Thine enemies,
have mercy on us.

O Jesus, the divine look of whose Adorable Face wounded
the heart of St. Peter with a dart of sorrow and love,
have mercy on us.

O Jesus, whose Adorable Face the pious Veronica
wiped on the way to Calvary,
have mercy on us.

O Jesus, whose Adorable Face was washed and anointed
by Mary and the holy women, and wrapped in a shroud,
have mercy on us.

O Jesus, whose Adorable Face was all resplendent
with glory and beauty on the day of Thy Resurrection,
have mercy on us.

O Jesus, whose Adorable Face is hidden in the Eucharist,
have mercy on us.

O Jesus, whose Adorable Face will appear at the end of time
in the clouds with great power and majesty,
have mercy on us.

O Jesus, whose Adorable Face
will cause the wicked to tremble,
have mercy on us.

O Jesus, whose Adorable Face
will fill the just with joy for all eternity,
have mercy on us.

Lamb of God, Who takest away the sins of the world,
Spare us O Lord.
Lamb of God, Who takest away the sins of the world,
Graciously hear us O Lord.
Lamb of God, Who takest away the sins of the world,
Have mercy on us.

LITANY OF THE HOLY FACE OF JESUS
In Reparation for Blasphemies - long version
(Manual of the Archconfraternity
of the Holy Face, 1887, p. 150-154)

O Adorable Face, which was adored with profound respect
by Mary and Joseph when they saw Thee
for the first time,
have mercy on us.

O Adorable Face, which in the Stable of Bethlehem didst
ravish with joy the angels, the shepherds and the Magi,
have mercy on us.

O Adorable Face, which in the Temple didst transpierce with
a dart of love the saintly old man Simeon
and the prophetess Anna,
have mercy on us.

O Adorable Face, which was bathed in tears
in Thy holy infancy,
have mercy on us.

O Adorable Face, which, when Thou didst appear in the
Temple at twelve years of age, didst fill with
admiration the Doctors of the law,
have mercy on us.

O Adorable Face, white with purity and ruddy with charity,
have mercy on us.

O Adorable Face, more beautiful than the sun, more lovely
than the moon, more brilliant than the stars,
have mercy on us.

O Adorable Face, fresher than the roses of spring,
have mercy on us.

O Adorable Face, more precious
than gold, silver and diamonds,
have mercy on us.

O Adorable Face, whose charms are so ravishing,
and whose grace is so attractive,
have mercy on us.

O Adorable Face, whose every feature
is characterized by nobility,
have mercy on us.

O Adorable Face, contemplated by angels,
have mercy on us.

O Adorable Face, sweet delectation of the Saints,
have mercy on us.

O Adorable Face, masterpiece of the Holy Ghost in which the
Eternal Father is well pleased,
have mercy on us.

O Adorable Face, delight of Mary and of Joseph,
have mercy on us.

O Adorable Face, ineffable mirror of the Divine Perfections,
have mercy on us.

O Adorable Face, whose beauty is
always ancient and always new,
have mercy on us.

O Adorable Face, which appeases the wrath of God,
have mercy on us.

O Adorable Face, which makest the devils tremble,
have mercy on us.

O Adorable Face, treasure of graces and of blessings,
have mercy on us.

O Adorable Face, exposed in the desert to
the inclemenc ies of the weather,
have mercy on us.

O Adorable Face, scorched with the heat of the sun and
bathed with sweat in Thy journeys,
have mercy on us.

O Adorable Face, whose expression is all divine,
have mercy on us.

O Adorable Face, whose modesty and sweetness
attracted both the just and sinners,
have mercy on us.

O Adorable Face, which gavest a holy kiss to the little
children, after having blessed them,
have mercy on us.

O Adorable Face, troubled and weeping
at the tomb of Lazarus,
have mercy on us.

O Adorable Face, brilliant as the sun,
and radiant with glory on Mount Tabor,
have mercy on us.

O Adorable Face, sorrowful at the sight of Jerusalem and
shedding tears on that ungrateful city,
have mercy on us.

O Adorable Face, bowed to the earth, in the garden of Olives,
and covered with confusion for our sins,
have mercy on us.

O Adorable Face, bathed in a bloody sweat,
have mercy on us.

O Adorable Face, kissed by the traitor Judas,
have mercy on us.

O Adorable Face, whose sanctity and majesty smote the
soldiers with fear and cast them to the ground,
have mercy on us.

O Adorable Face, struck by a vile servant,
shamefully blindfolded, and profaned by the
sacrilegious hands of Thine enemies,
have mercy on us.

O Adorable Face, defiled with spittle
and bruised by innumerable buffets and blows,
have mercy on us.

O Adorable Face, whose Divine look wounded the heart of
Peter, with a dart of sorrow and love,
have mercy on us.

O Adorable Face humbled for us at the tribunals of Jerusalem,
have mercy on us.

O Adorable Face, which didst preserve Thy serenity when
Pilate pronounced the fatal sentence,
have mercy on us.

O Adorable Face, covered with sweat and blood, and falling
in the mire under the heavy weight of the Cross,
have mercy on us.

O Adorable Face, worthy of all our respect,
veneration and worship,
have mercy on us.

O Adorable Face, wiped with a veil by a pious woman,
on the road to Calvary,
have mercy on us.

O Adorable Face, raised on the instrument
of most shameful punishment,
have mercy on us.

O Adorable Face, whose brow was crowned with thorns,
have mercy on us.

O Adorable Face, whose eyes were filled with tears of blood,
have mercy on us.

O Adorable Face, whose mouth was poured gall and vinegar,
have mercy on us.

O Adorable Face, whose hair and beard
were plucked out by the executioners,
have mercy on us.

O Adorable Face, which was made like to that of a leper,
have mercy on us.

O Adorable Face, whose incomparable beauty was obscured
under the dreadful cloud of the sins of the world,
have mercy on us.

O Adorable Face, covered with the sad shades of death,
have mercy on us.

O Adorable Face, washed and anointed by Mary and the holy
women and wrapped in a shroud,
have mercy on us.

O Adorable Face, enclosed in the sepulcher,
have mercy on us.

O Adorable Face, all resplendent with glory and beauty
on the day of the Resurrection,
have mercy on us.

O Adorable Face, all dazzling with light
at the moment of Thy Ascension,
have mercy on us.

O Adorable Face, hidden in the Eucharist,
have mercy on us.

O Adorable Face, which wilt appear at the end of time in the
clouds with great power and majesty,
have mercy on us.

O Adorable Face, which wilt cause sinners to tremble,
have mercy on us.

O Adorable Face, which wilt fill the just
with joy for all eternity,
have mercy on us.

Lamb of God, who takest away the sins of the world,
spare us, O Lord.
Lamb of God, who takest away the sins of the world,
graciously hear us.
Lamb of God, who takest away the sins of the world,
have mercy on us.

PRAYER OF REPARATION TO THE HOLY FACE
*(Manual of the Archconfraternity
of the Holy Face, 1887, p. 170)*

Lord Jesus! After having contemplated Thy features,
disfigured by grief; after having meditated upon Thy
Passion with compunction and love, how can our hearts
help being inflamed with a holy hatred of sin, which even
now, still outrages Thy Adorable Face? But, not allowing
ourselves to be content with mere compassion, give us

grace to follow Thee so closely on this new Calvary, that the opprobrium destined for Thee may rebound upon us, O Jesus, and that we may at least have some small share in the expiation of sin. Amen.

OFFERING OF THE HOLY FACE TO THE ETERNAL FATHER
*(Manual of the Archconfraternity
of the Holy Face, 1887, p. 171)*

Almighty God, Eternal Father, contemplate the Face of Thy Son, our Lord Jesus Christ. We present it to Thee with confidence for the glory of Thy Holy Name, for the exaltation of Thy holy Church, and for the salvation of the world. Most merciful Advocate, He opens His mouth to plead our cause; listen to His cries, behold His tears, O my God, and Thou wilt be touched with compassion towards the poor sinners who ask of Thee grace and mercy. Amen.

PRAYERS OF LEO DUPONT
*(Manual of the Archconfraternity
of the Holy Face, 1887, p. 172-175)*

1.   O Savior Jesus! At the sight of Thy most Holy Face, disfigured by grief, and at the sight of Thy Sacred Heart so full of love, I cry out with Saint Augustine: Lord Jesus, impress upon my heart Thy sacred wounds, that I may read therein at once Thy sorrow and Thy love; Thy sorrow, in order to suffer every affliction for Thee; Thy love, in order for Thee to despise every other love. Amen.

2.   Lord Jesus! When presenting ourselves before Thy adorable Face to entreat Thee for the graces of which we have need, we beseech Thee, above all things, so to order the interior dispositions of our hearts, that we may never refuse Thee aught that Thou Thyself askest of us every day, through Thy holy commandments and by Thy divine inspirations. Amen.

3.   Be merciful to us, O my God! Do not reject our prayers, when in the midst of our afflictions, we call upon Thy Holy Name and seek with love and confidence Thy Adorable Face. Amen.

We thank Thee, O Lord, for all Thy benefits, and we entreat Thee to engrave in our hearts feelings of love and of gratitude, putting upon our lips songs of thanksgiving to Thy eternal praise. Amen

PRAYER
THAT LEO DUPONT USED WHEN
ANNOINTING THE SICK WITH OIL
(Manual of the Archconfraternity
of the Holy Face, 1887, p. 174)

Unctiones sanitates conficiat et perficiat ipse Deus. In nominee Patris, etc.

In English: May the Lord himself deign, together with us, to anoint this sick person and to restore him to health, in the name of the Father, etc.

Or else: May the holy Name of Jesus, of Mary and of Joseph be known, blessed and glorified throughout the whole earth. Amen.

RESOLUTION TO CONFESS OUR SINS
BEFORE ASKING FOR A CURE
(Manual of the Archconfraternity
of the Holy Face, 1887, p. 174-175)

Thy word, Lord Jesus, granted to the happy paralytic, in the Gospel, the remission of his sins, before Thou said to him: Arise. (Mark, II, 2.) Therefore, I, a miserable sinner, knowing and firmly believing, that Thou hast given to Thy priests' power to remit sins, resolve to descend at once into the sacred bath of penitence, before calling upon the eyes of Thy mercy, to look upon my corporal infirmities. Then, submitting myself, heart and soul, to Thy most holy will, I will await, in peace, O Lord, the accomplishment of my wishes here on earth, with the hope of contemplating, blessing and praising Thy adorable Face for ever and ever in heaven. Amen.

PRAYERS OF REPARATION

Adorable Face of Jesus, which was so mercifully bowed
down on the Cross on the day of Thy Passion
for the salvation of the world!
Once more today in pity,
bend down towards us poor sinners. Cast upon us a
glance of compassion and give us Thy peace. Amen.

Be merciful to us, O my God! Do not reject our prayers,
when in the midst of our afflictions, we call upon
Thy Holy Name and seek with love and confidence
Thy Adorable Face. Amen.

Prayer of Pius IX
*(Manual of the Archconfraternity
of the Holy Face, 1887, p. 177)*

O my Jesus! Cast upon us a look of mercy; turn Thy Face towards each one of us, even as Thou didst turn to Veronica, not that we may see it with the eyes of our body, for we do not deserve to do so, but turn it towards our hearts, that, being sustained by Thee, we may ever draw from that powerful source, the vigor necessary to enable us to wage the combats we have to undergo.

Amen.

Aspiration
(Sr. Marie de Saint-Pierre)

Eternal Father, we offer Thee the adorable Face of Thy well beloved Son for the honor and glory of Thy holy Name and for the salvation of all men. Amen.

Prayer to the Holy Face
(St. Therese of the Child Jesus and of the Holy Face)

O Adorable Face of Jesus, the only Beauty that captivates my heart, deign to imprint in me your Divine Likeness so that you may not behold the soul of your little bride without seeing Yourself in her.

O my Beloved, for love of you, I accept not seeing here below the gentleness of your Look nor feeling the ineffable kiss of your Mouth, but I beg you to inflame me with your love so that it may consume me rapidly and soon bring me into your presence. Amen.

PRAYER OF VENERATION
(St. Therese of the Child Jesus and of the Holy Face)

O Jesus, who in Thy bitter Passion didst become "the most abject of men, a man of sorrows", I venerate Thy Sacred Face whereon there once did shine the beauty and sweetness of the Godhead; but now it has become for me as if it were the face of a leper! Nevertheless, under those disfigured features, I recognize Thy infinite Love and I am consumed with the desire to love Thee and make Thee loved by all men.

The tears which well up abundantly in Thy sacred eyes appear to me as so many precious pearls that I love to gather up, in order to purchase the souls of poor sinners by means of their infinite value. O Jesus, whose adorable face ravishes my heart, I implore Thee to fix deep within me Thy divine image and to set me on fire with Thy Love, that I may be found worthy to come to the contemplation of Thy glorious Face in Heaven. Amen.

PRAYER OF BLESSED MARIA-PIERINA

O Blessed Face of my kind Savior, by the tender love and piercing sorrow of Our Lady as she beheld you in your cruel Passion, grant us to share in this intense sorrow and love so as to fulfill the holy will of God to the utmost of our ability. Amen.

OFFERING OF THE INFINITE MERITS
OF OUR LORD JESUS CHRIST TO GOD THE FATHER
IN ORDER TO APPEASE HIS JUSTICE
AND DRAW DOWN HIS MERCY UPON US
(Manual of the Archconfraternity
of the Holy Face, 1887, p. 222-225)

Eternal Father, turn away Thine angry gaze from our guilty people, whose face has become hideous in Thine eyes, and look upon the Face of Thy Son which we offer to Thee. It is Thy well beloved Son in whom Thou art well pleased. Listen we beseech Thee to the voice of his blood and of his wounds which call for mercy from Thee.

Eternal Father, look upon the incarnation of Jesus, Thy divine Son, and his sojourn in the womb of his divine Mother. We offer them to Thee for the honor and glory of Thy holy Name and for the salvation of our country.

Eternal Father, look upon the birth of Jesus in the stable at Bethlehem and the mysteries of his most Holy Infancy. We offer them to Thee…

Eternal Father, look upon the poor, hidden laborious life of Jesus at Nazareth. We offer it to Thee…

Eternal Father, look upon the baptism of Jesus and his retreat of forty days in the desert. We offer them to Thee…

Eternal Father, look upon the journeys, the vigils, the prayers, the miracles and the teachings of Jesus. We offer them to Thee…

Eternal Father, look upon the last supper Jesus partook of with his disciples washing their feet, and instituting the august sacrament of the Eucharist. We offer them to Thee…

134

Eternal Father, look upon the agony of Jesus in the garden of Olives and the bloody sweat which covered his body and ran down to the ground. We offer them to Thee…

Eternal Father, look upon the outrages which Jesus underwent before his judges and his condemnation to death. We offer them to Thee…

Eternal Father, look upon Jesus, laden with his Cross and proceeding to the place where he was to be immolated. We offer him to Thee…

Eternal Father, look upon Jesus crucified between two thieves, and made to drink gall and vinegar, blasphemed by the Jews, and dying in order to repair Thy glory and to save the world. We offer him to Thee…

Eternal Father, look upon the five wounds of Jesus. We offer them to Thee…

Eternal Father, look upon the sacred Head of Jesus, crowned with thorns. We offer it to Thee…

Eternal Father, look upon the adorable Face of Jesus, wounded with blows, covered with spittle, with dust, with sweat and with blood. We offer it to Thee…

Eternal Father, look upon the adorable Body of Jesus, taken down from the Cross. We offer it to Thee…

Eternal Father, look upon the heart, the soul and the divinity of Jesus, the holy victim, who when dying triumphed over sin. We offer them to Thee…

Look, O Eternal Father, on all that Jesus Christ, Thy only Son, did during the thirty-three years of his mortal life, in order to accomplish the work of our redemption; look upon all the mysteries of that most holy life. We offer them to Thee…

Look, O Eternal Father, on all the desires, all the thoughts, the words, the actions, the virtues, the perfections, the prayers of Jesus Christ, as well as upon all his sufferings and humiliations. We offer them to Thee…

Look, O Eternal Father, on the crib and the swaddling clothes used at the birth of Jesus. We offer them to Thee…

Look, O Eternal Father, on the Cross, the nails, the crown of thorns, the reed, the bloody scourges, the pillar, the lance, the sepulcher, the holy shroud, and all the instruments used in the Passion of Jesus. We offer them to Thee, for the salvation of our country and for the entire world. Amen.

LITTLE SCAPULAR OF THE HOLY FACE
The Little Scapular comes to us from Leo Dupont
(Manual of the Archconfraternity
of the Holy Face, 1887, p. 232-233)

The scapular of the Holy Face is a small picture of that adorable Face, printed upon linen, which the faithful wear for devotion as a testimony of love towards our Lord and a preservative against temptations and the dangers of the soul and body.

It may be fastened upon the scapular of our Lady of mount Carmel or upon any other which is worn; it is not necessary to have recourse to a priest in order to receive it, and there is no liturgical form to be complied with; when taking it to wear, no other obligation is contracted than that of wearing it in a spirit of faith and of reparation. It is a small copy of the veil of Saint Veronica which has touched the great relic at Rome.

LITTLE SACHET OR THE LITTLE GOSPEL
Revealed to Sister Marie St. Pierre
(Manual of the Archconfraternity
of the Holy Face, 1887, p. 243-244)

This devotional consists of a leaflet on which is printed the gospel of the Circumcision, which is short, and in which is made mention of the Name of Jesus, given to the Savior. On the same leaflet is engraved, at the top of it, the figure of the Divine Child and the initials of His adorable Name, and below the Gospel, some pious invocations calculated to excite confidence in the Name of Jesus, together with the lines:

When Jesus was named,
Vanquished Satan was disarmed.

The leaflet is folded in two and enclosed in a little piece of stuff, on which is embroidered a Cross with the Sacred Heart, so that it resembles a medal suitable to be worn on the person.

There is no other blessing needed, in order to receive it, than that which is attached to the Holy Name of Jesus. In honor of the five letters of this divine Name, and by virtue of the five wounds, our Lord has promised to grant special graces to those who shall embrace this devotion with faith and piety:

1st to preserve them from lightening.

2nd to preserve them from the cunning malice of the devil.

3rd to preserve them from sudden and unprovided death.

4th to enable them to walk readily along the path of virtue.

5th to grant to them final perseverance.

Our lord is pleased to manifest the power of his Holy Name by many other spiritual and temporal graces: conversions, cures, etc. The sachet is principally employed with success in the case of dying sinners.

This devotion to the Holy Name of Jesus is attached to the great work of the Reparation of blasphemies and to that of the Holy Face.

PRAYER OF POPE INNOCENT III (1207)

O God, who in the image impressed on Veronica's Veil
wanted to leave your memorial for us who are sealed in
the light of your face. We beg you to obtain for us
through the merits of your passion and cross, that as we
now on earth venerate and adore the very mystery of its
likeness, so we may see it face to face
unto salvation when the Judge comes. Amen.

PRAYER TO OUR LORD JESUS CHRIST
*The true repairer of the outrages
committed against the glory of his Father*

O Jesus! At the sight of the blasphemers of the sacred
Name of God, we beseech Thee to repeat with us the
prayer Thou didst once address to Thy divine Father, and
which has been given to us by Saint John, Thy beloved
disciple: *Father, glorify Thy Name.* Then, O divine Jesus,
came a voice from heaven saying: *I have glorified it already,
and I will glorify it again.*

May that voice resound throughout the earth, we
entreat Thee by Thy sacred wounds and by Thy adorable
Face! As for us, forgetting at this moment our own
interests, in order to defend the glory of Thy Father's
Name, we will keep in mind the three first petitions of the
prayer Thou Thyself hast taught us: *Our Father, who art in
heaven, hallowed be thy Name: thy kingdom come: thy will be
done on earth as it is in heaven.* Amen.

139

PRAYER IN HONOR OF THE HOLY FACE
(Devotion to the Holy Face
at St. Peter's of the Vatican, Janvier, 1888)

O God, who hast shed upon us the light of Thy Face, and who, by means of Veronica, hast willed to leave us Thy image impressed upon her veil, as an eternal warrant of Thy love, grant us, by Thy Passion and Thy Cross, grace to venerate Thee, to adore Thee, and to glorify Thee now upon earth, whilst contemplating Thee as in the mirror of an enigma, in such a manner that we may not fear to look upon Thee face to face, when Thou comest Lord Jesus Christ, to judge us in the clouds of heaven. Amen

God Eternal and Almighty, who by a special grace didst cause the precious features of Thy divine Face to shine upon Thy people assembled together to honor it, grant them the pardon of their sins, and govern the words, actions, senses and the faculties of those who confide in Thy mercy. Amen.

PRAYER
*(Veronica, or the Holy Face of Our Lord Jesus Christ,
An Historical Notice of the Most Holy Relic, 1870)*

Make glad, O Lord, the face of Thy servant, and draw our souls from perdition, that, being protected by the contemplation of Your adorable Face, we may trample under foot all carnal desires, and behold You without fear, face to face, when You will come in the clouds of heaven, with power and majesty to judge us. Through Christ our Lord. Amen.

PRAYER
*(Veronica, or the Holy Face of Our Lord Jesus Christ,
An Historical Notice of the Most Holy Relic, 1870)*

O Adorable Face of my Jesus, so mercifully bowed down on the tree of the Cross, on the day of Thy Passion, for the salvation of the world! Today again through compassion incline to us poor sinners, let fall on us one look of compassion, and receive us with a kiss of peace. Amen.

Sacred Heart of Jesus, have mercy on us.
Sit nomen Domini benedictum! Amen.

The Feast Day of the Holy Face:
Shrove Tuesday (the day before Ash Wednesday)
Formally declared by Pope Pius XII in 1958

Patron Saints and Protectors of the Holy Face:
St. Michael, St. Louis, St. Martin & St. Veronica

Prayer to Obtain the Settlement of all Our Needs

Oh, Eternal Father, since it has pleased our Divine Savior to reveal to mankind in our present century the power residing in His Holy Face, we now avail ourselves of this treasure in our great needs. Since our Savior Himself promised that by offering to You, oh Eternal Father, the Holy Face disfigured in the Passion, we can procure the settlement of all our affairs, and that nothing whatsoever will be refused us, we now come before Your Throne.

Offering to You, oh God, this adorable Countenance, disfigured with painful bruises and covered with shame and confusion, we beg through the merits of this Holy Face to obtain these, our pressing needs.

Grant us pardon, Eternal Father, for the worst crimes of our age, which are atheism, blasphemy, and the desecration of Your holy days. May this offering of the Holy Face of our Savior before Your Throne obtain for us deliverance from these evils.

Send us, oh God, many vocations to the priesthood and to the religious life, so that by their prayers, their works, and their sacrifices, they may spread the blessings of Your Church and confound Your enemies. Amen.

PROMISES OF OUR LORD JESUS CHRIST
IN FAVOR OF THOSE WHO HONOR HIS HOLY FACE
As Our Lord revealed to Sr. Mary of St. Peter

1. All who honor My Face in a spirit of reparation will by so doing perform the office of the pious Veronica. According to the care they take in making reparation to My Face, disfigured by blasphemers, so will I take care of their souls which have been disfigured by sin. My Face is the seal of the Divinity, which has the virtue of reproducing in souls the image of God.

2. Those who by words, prayers or writing defend My cause in this Work of Reparation, I will defend before My Father, and will give them My Kingdom.

3. By offering My Face to My Eternal Father, nothing will be refused, and the conversion of many sinners will be obtained.

4. By My Holy Face, they will work wonders, appease the anger of God and draw down mercy on sinners.

5. As in a kingdom they can procure all that is desired with a coin stamped with the King's effigy, so in the Kingdom of Heaven they will obtain all they desire with the precious coin of My Face.

6. Those who on earth contemplate the wounds of My Face shall in Heaven behold it radiant with glory.

7. They will receive in their souls a bright and constant irradiation of My Divinity, that by their likeness to My Face they shall shine with particular splendor in Heaven.

8. I will defend them, I will preserve them, and I assure them of Final Perseverance.

Source Materials & References

_____

Manual of the Archconfraternity of the Holy Face followed by *The Little Office of the Holy Name of God,* the REV. ABBE JANVIER, Dean of the metropolitan Chapter of Tours, Priest of the Holy Face, translated from the French by Mrs. A. R. Bennett, Tours, the Oratory of the Holy Face, original manual of 1887, Public Domain. (**APPROBATION** from the Archbishop of Tours, France, April 15, 1886)

The Manual of the Holy Face, A.M.P., printed from the original Manual of the Archconfraternity of the Holy Face of 1887, includes 1885 Manual of the Confraternity of the Holy Face, published by St Paul Press, Dallas, TX, 2018.

The Golden Arrow, the Autobiography and Revelations of Sister Mary of St. Peter on Devotion to the Holy Face of Jesus, edited by DOROTHY SCALLAN, translated by Fr. Emeric B. Scallan, S.T.B., Public Domain, published by St. Jerome Library Press, 2019. (**IMPRIMATUR:** Francis Cardinal Spellman, Archbishop of New York, March 15, 1954)

God Demands Reparation, the Holy Man of Tours, the Life of Leo Dupont, Apostle of the Holy Face Devotion, by DOROTHY SCALLAN, edited by Rev. Emeric B. Scallan, S.T.B., Public Domain, published by St Jerome Library Press, 2021. (**IMPRIMATUR:** Francis Cardinal Spellman, Archbishop of New York, December 13, 1951)

The Holy Man of Tours, or, The Life of Leon Papin-Dupont, Who Died at Tours in the Odor of Sanctity, March 18, 1876, by PIERRE DESIRE JANVIER, translated by M. L'Abbe Pierre Desire' Janvier, Priest of the Holy Face, originally published by John Murphy & Co., 1882, Public Domain, published by Franklin Classics, an imprint of Creative Media Partners.

The Autobiography of Therese of Lisieux, the Story of A Soul, translated by Michael Day, Public Domain, published by Dover Publications, Inc., 2022. (**IMPRIMATUR:** E. Morrogh Bernard, Vic. Gen. Westmonastery, DIE 27A, January 1958)

The Story of A Soul, St. Therese of Lisieux, translated and edited by Robert J. Edmonson, CJ, Public Domain, published by Paraclete Press, 9th printing 2017

Autobiography of St. Therese of Lisieux, the complete and authorized text of "L'Histoire d'une Ame", newly translated by Ronald Knox, a translation of *St. Therese de l' Enfant Jesus — Manuscrits Autobiographiques* (Lisieux, Carmel de Lisieux, 1957), Public Domain, published by P.J. Kenedy & Sons, 1958

The Whole World Will Love Me, the Life of St. Therese of the Child Jesus and of the Holy Face, by DOROTHY SCALLAN, edited by Fr. Emeric B. Scallan, S.T.B., first published by The William Frederick Press, New York, 1954, published by Tan Books and Publishers, Inc., 2005. (**IMPRIMATUR:** Francis Cardinal Spellman, Archbishop of New York, July 28, 1953)

The Story of Sister Maria Pierina De Micheli, Missionary – Messenger of the Holy Face of Jesus, by Sister Maria Ildefonsa Rigamonti, 1958. (**IMPRIMATUR:** J. Schiavini, Vic. Gen., December 18, 1957)

Veronica, or, The Holy Face of Our Lord Jesus Christ, An Historical Notice of this Most Holy Relic of the Vatican Basilica of St. Peter, London, published by Thomas Richardson and Son, 1870. Public Domain.

The Devotion to The Holy Face at St. Peter's of the Vatican and in Other Celebrated Places, by the REV. ABBE JANVIER, 1888. Public Domain. (**IMPRIMATUR:** Charles, Archbishop of Tours, November 16, 1888)

Life of Sister Mary St. Peter Carmelite of Tours, by M. LABBE JANVIER, director of the Priests of the Holy Face, Revised Addition 1884. Public Domain. (**APPROBATION** from the Archbishop of Tours, 1884)

Archives Du Carmel De Lisieux, Last Words with Celine (Sr. Genevieve), 1897, www.archives-carmel-lisieux.fr

What is the Shroud of Turin? Facts & History Everyone Should Know, article by Myra Adams and Russ Breult, Nov. 8, 2019, published by Christianity.com

The Devotion to the Holy Face as Revealed to Blessed Maria Pierina, faithfully copied from Mother Pierina's biogrophy, with **Ecclesiastical Approbation**, printed by the Holy Face Association, Champlain, NY, and Montreal, Quebec, Canada, www.holyface.com

RECOMMENDED READING

The Manual of the Holy Face, A.M.P., printed from the original Manual of the Archconfraternity of the Holy Face of 1887, publisher: St. Paul Press, Dallas, TX., 2018 - www.amazon.com

The Golden Arrow, the Autobiography and Revelations of Sister Mary of St. Peter on Devotion to the Holy Face of Jesus, edited by DOROTHY SCALLAN, publisher: St. Jerome Library Press, Elkhorn, WI, 2019. - www.StJeromeLibrary.org

God Demands Reparation, the Holy Man of Tours, the Life of Leo Dupont, Apostle of the Holy Face Devotion, by DOROTHY SCALLAN, publisher: St Jerome Library Press, Elkhorn, WI, 2021. – www.StJeromeLibrary.org

The Autobiography of Therese of Lisieux, the Story of a Soul, translated by Michael Day, publisher: Dover Publications, Inc., Mineola, NY., 2022
- www.doverpublications.com

The Whole World Will Love Me, the Life of St. Therese of the Child Jesus and of the Holy Face, by DOROTHY SCALLAN, publisher: Tan Books and Publishers, Inc., Rockford, IL, 2005.
- www.tanbooks.com

Sister Saint-Pierre and the Work of Reparation, A Brief History, by the Very Rev. Pierre Desire' Janvier, Director of the Priests of the Holy Face at Tours, translated by Miss Mary Hoffman, 1885, publisher: Forgotten Books. London, England, 2018. This is a Classic Reprint.
- www.forgottenbooks.com
- www.amazon.com

NOTES

Printed in Great Britain
by Amazon

44012741R00086